CW00853734

AN INTRODUCTION TO IRISH RESEARCH

Irish ancestry: A beginner's guide

SECOND EDITION

Bill Davis

Published by
The Federation of Family History Societies (Publications) Ltd
The Benson Room, Birmingham and Midland Institute
Margaret Street, Birmingham B3 3BS

First published 1992
Second edition 1994
Revised 1998

ISBN 1 86006 074 9

Printed and bound by Oxuniprint, Great Clarendon Street, Oxford OX2 6DP

ACKNOWLEDGEMENTS

Numerous people and organisations have given their time to help me with the various editions of this book and I am grateful to all of them.

For the preparation of the first edition, my special thanks go to Paul Gorry of the Association of Professional Genealogists in Ireland (APGI), Dr. Stephen Taylor, Jean Tooke and Hillary Marshall of the Association of Genealogists and Record Agents (AGRA) and Ettie Pullman of the Australasian Association of Genealogists and Record Agents (AAGRA) for information about their organisations and advice to prospective clients; J. Gordon Read, Curator of Archives, Merseyside Maritime Museum for his kind advice; John C. McTernan, County Sligo Librarian, for allowing me to quote from his book; the General Register Office and National Archives, Dublin, for permission to reproduce material; the Controller of Her Majesty's Stationery Office for permission to use extracts from *British Parliamentary Papers*; Maeve Catford, Brian Christmas, Peter and Rosemary Cleaver of the West Surrey Family History Society, Michael McGovern and Peter Manning of the Irish Genealogical Research Society for answering my queries, reading the manuscript and offering suggestions.

For the preparation of the second edition, I wish to thank Donal F. Begley, Chief Herald of Ireland, Aideen Ireland, Archivist of the National Archives, Ken Bruce and Aileen McClintock of the Public Record Office of Northern Ireland, Dr. Patricia Donlon, Director of the National Library of Ireland, Patrick Scanlon, Record Keeper at the Valuation Office, Joan Phillipson of the Association of Ulster Genealogists and Record Agents (AUGRA), Brian O'Loughlin, Registry of Deeds, Elder Horsley of the Hyde Park Family History Centre, Alexandra Nichol, Susan Healy and Ruth Paley of the Public Record Office, Stella Colwell, Publicity Officer of the Society of Genealogists, Janet Koss, Service Development Unit, the British Library, Jill Allbrooke, Information Officer, the British Library's Newspaper Library, Mary Casteleyn, Librarian of the Irish Genealogical Research Society, Irene Fullerton of the Genealogical Society of Victoria, and the staff of the Library of Congress for information about their respective archives. Also Marion Brackpool, Secretary of the East Surrey FHS, Kate Press, editor of *The Genealogist*, Christine Smith, editor of *Generation*, and Sheila Quinn, Marketing Executive of Leader Tourism Promotions for permission to quote from their respective publications. I am also grateful to Timothy Brabants for his contribution to the artwork on the front cover.

Irish genealogical research is no longer confined to Ireland, the presence of millions of Irish descendants worldwide making it a subject of international interest. Many of them wish to trace their roots but are convinced that the task is impossible, or so difficult that it should not be attempted. To them, and to Irish descendants everywhere, this book is dedicated.

On two visits to Ireland,
we received wonderful
hospitality wherever we went
.... time was the most valuable
thing given to us ....

A.S. Allaby

FOREWORD TO THIS REVISED EDITION

Ancestral research is blossoming around the world together with an increase in literature on the subject of genealogy. There was, however, little about Ireland and the need for a basic guide on the subject of Irish genealogical research was paramount. In 1992, the first edition of this book fulfilled that need. The following year, a review of research guides was conducted in the magazine *Irish Roots* by Paul Gorry. *An Introduction to Irish Research* took first place in the 'guidance' category, shared first place for 'readability' and second place overall with two other guides. The second edition, whilst adhering to the introductory theme, explored the subject in greater depth, taking account of new developments in the field of Irish research. A chapter on sources was added and the existing chapter on records extended. There were additional appendices, and a greater emphasis was placed upon the availability of records outside Ireland. This revised edition takes account of further developments in Irish research and some updating of sources.

The beauty of this book is that it can be taken to Ireland for reference purposes or used for guidance during postal research. Either way, it is an indispensable handbook for Irish descendants worldwide.

CONTENTS

INTRODUCTION

The introduction to the first edition of this book was as follows.

Worldwide genealogical research

In recent years, the popularity of genealogical research has increased dramatically, particularly in countries with a history of immigration. Research organisations have been formed and an abundance of literature now exists to satisfy the needs of family historians. Much of this material refers to the immigration of settlers whose descendants are now striving to discover their origins. One of the largest groups of migrants came from Ireland, a small country on the north-west fringe of Europe whose population has been emigrating for centuries to all parts of the world. Today, that migration continues and conservative estimates now put the number of Irish descendants around the world at between 40 and 70 million.

Records of immigration

Most countries have, at some time or other, been host to Irish immigration, particularly France and Spain, where thousands of Irish settled as a result of historical events. But the countries that experienced most immigration were undoubtedly Britain, North America, Canada, and to a lesser extent, Australia and New Zealand. This has resulted in a plethora of material (census returns, civil registration documents, etc., in which the Irish are clearly identified. But such is the nature of the subject, that the trail inevitably leads back to Ireland, a shortage of records, and more often than not, a halt to one's research.

Civil war in Ireland

The main reason for this is that, in 1922, during the Irish Civil War, the Public Record Office in Dublin was badly damaged, and records that would have been useful to researchers were destroyed. Other material survived, but the 'destructions' gave rise to the widely held belief that everything was destroyed and research today is therefore impossible.

Ancestral tourists

During recent years in Ireland, efforts have been made to alleviate this situation by combining genealogical research with tourism, showing visitors their ancestral homes, and organising seminars and courses around the country. Despite this, many people still find Irish family history, and in particular Irish records, confusing for little effort has been made to acquaint them, in simple terms, with the basic principles of Irish research.

Bringing the reader up to date

That introduction is still relevant. With more people becoming interested in their Irish roots, the greater their need for knowledge not only about ancestors, but why Irish research is so difficult and whether anything was being done about it. That first edition answered many of the problems that had discouraged Irish research and by guiding readers along the correct path enabled them to avoid many pitfalls. The second edition continued that tradition. This revised edition, taking into account further developments, is now essential reading for the understanding of Irish genealogical research.

Chapter 1

THE BASICS OF IRISH RESEARCH

Preparing for research

When preparing for a holiday, arrangements are usually made well in advance, brochures/timetables are studied, airline tickets obtained and accommodation arranged. These are logical steps to take, the object being to avoid difficulties later; and it is at the preparatory stage of Irish research that problems begin. It is not a case of preparing for travel, but acquiring in advance a knowledge of Irish history, geography, and genealogy. A basic knowledge of certain essentials will help to save time and money, yet family historians travel, sometimes thousands of miles, to Ireland in search of their ancestry, with little idea of how to begin. The first rule therefore, is to *know and understand the basics of Irish research.*

Getting to grips with the basics

Some researchers are unfamiliar with Ireland's geography and it is a good idea to examine a map showing its counties. You will also discover that Ireland is sub-divided in an unusual way: provinces into counties; counties into baronies; baronies into parishes and parishes into townlands. Figures 1.1–1.3 show this arrangement. Family historians are frequently unaware of this structure, yet such knowledge is absolutely essential for locating, examining and understanding surviving records, most of which are grouped within those categories.

The workman's tools

The Townland Index

A vital tool for use during your research is the *Alphabetical Index to The Townlands and Towns of Ireland,* more commonly known as the *Townland Index.* Compiled during the 19th and early 20th centuries after certain censuses (see Chapter 6), it lists all the baronies, parishes, towns, villages and townlands that existed at the time. Its value to family historians lies in the fact that it enables them to pinpoint locations with accuracy, which, if accomplished during the early stages of research, will help to save much time and expense. *The Townland Index* can be found in the National Archives (NA), the Public Record Office of Northern Ireland (PRONI), the National Library of Ireland (NLI), and other sources around Ireland. It will also be found nestling among the more than 7,000 volumes of the *British Parliamentary Papers* in the British Library (BL), the Public Record Office (PRO), and the Irish Genealogical Research Society (IGRS) in London.

Now this is all very convenient for researchers in Ireland and Britain, but what about family historians elsewhere? The news is encouraging. The 1861 *Townland Index*, based upon the census of 1851, has been republished in the United States by the Genealogical Publishing Company, Baltimore under the longer title: *The General Alphabetical Index to The Townlands and Towns, Parishes and Baronies of Ireland.* This brings an aspect of Irish research closer to family historians, for now that it has been republished, the *Townland Index* may be within reach of Irish descendants worldwide through bookshops and libraries.

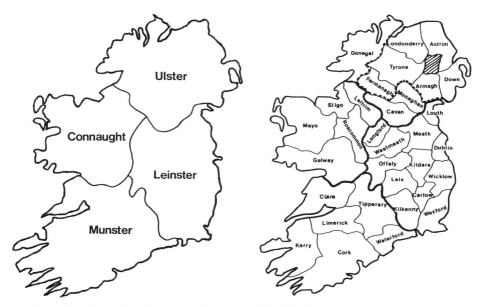

Fig. 1.1. Map showing the four provinces of Ireland.

Fig. 1.2. Map showing the provinces of Ireland and counties contained in each. The dotted line encompasses the six counties known today as Northern Ireland.

PROVINCE

|

COUNTIES

|

BARONIES

|

PARISHES

|

TOWNLANDS

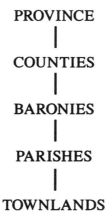

Fig. 1.3. Diagram showing the sub-division of provinces and counties.

CENSUS OF IRELAND,
1871.

GENERAL ALPHABETICAL INDEX

TO THE

TOWNLANDS AND TOWNS OF IRELAND,

With the Number of the Sheet of the Ordnance Survey Maps on which they appear ; the Area in Statute Acres of each Townland ; the County, Barony, Parish, Poor Law Union, and Poor Law Electoral Division in which it is situated ; and the Volume and Page of the Census of 1871, Part I., giving the Population, Houses, and Valuation.

** The names of Towns are printed in SMALL CAPITALS, and those of *Islands* which are not Townlands in *Italics*.

No. of Sheet of the Ordnance Survey Maps.	Names of Townlands and Towns.	Area in Statute Acres.			County.	Barony.	Parish.	Poor Law Union.	Poor Law Electoral Division.	Census of 1871. Part I.	
		A.	R.	P.						Vol.	Page
34	Abartagh . . .	34	2	32	Waterford .	Decies-within-Drum	Clashmore .	Youghal . .	Clashmore . .	II.	880
97	Abberanville . .	24	0	29	Galway . .	Athenry . .	Kiltullagh . .	Loughrea . .	Raford . .	IV.	19
93	Abbernadoorny . .	62	2	29	Donegal . .	Banagh . .	Killymard . .	Donegal . .	Donegal. .	III.	366
68	Abbert . .	178	3	30	} Galway . .	Tiaquin . .	Monivea . .	Tuam . .	Abbey East .	IV.	109
58, 59	Abbert Demesne .	1,293	3	21							
4	Abbeville . .	943	2	7	Tipperary, N.R. .	Ormond Lower	Lorrha . .	Borrisokane	Lorrha East. .	II.	716
118	Abbey . . .	27	0	22	Cork, W.R. . .	Bantry . .	Kilmocomoge .	Bantry . .	Bantry . .	II.	214
16,117,125	Abbey . . .	334	8	26	Galway . .	Leitrim . .	Ballynakill . .	Portumna .	Tynagh . .	IV.	75
65	Abbey . . .	875	3	7	Galway . .	Tiaquin . .	Abbeyknockmoy	Tuam . .	Abbey West .	IV.	104
56	Abbey . . .	222	3	21	Limerick . .	Coshlea . .	Kilfyn . .	Kilmallock .	Kilfyn . .	II.	572
13	Abbeycartron . . (a)	—			Longford . .	Longford . .	Templemichael .	Longford . .	Longford . .	I.	527
16	Abbeycartron . .	32	1	3	Roscommon . .	Roscommon . .	Elphin . .	Strokestown .	Elphin . .	IV.	467
6,19,22,23	Abbeyderg . .	867	2	21	Longford . .	Moydow . .	Taghsheenod .	Ballymahon .	Kilcommock .	I.	530
31	ABBEYDORNEY T. .	—			Kerry . .	Clanmaurice .	O'Dorney . .	Tralee . .	Abbeydorney .	II.	423
4	Abbeydown . .	454	3	6	Wexford . .	Scarawalsh .	Moyacomb . .	Shillelagh .	Moyacomb .	I.	1000
3	Abbey East . .	301	0	12	Clare . .	Burren . .	Abbey . .	Ballyvaghan .	Abbey . .	II.	74
47	Abbeyfarm . .	55	1	12	Limerick . .	Kilmallock .	St. Peter's & St. Paul's	Kilmallock .	Kilmallock .	II.	584
47, 51	Abbeyfeale East . .	1,350	3	23	Limerick . .	Glenquin . .	Abbeyfeale . .	Newcastle .	Abbeyfeale .	II.	577
42	ABBEYFEALE T. . .	—			Limerick . .	Glenquin . .	Abbeyfeale . .	Newcastle .	Abbeyfeale .	II.	578
42	Abbeyfeale West . .	718	2	4	Limerick . .	Glenquin . .	Abbeyfeale . .	Newcastle .	Abbeyfeale .	II.	577
56	Abbeyfield . .	18	0	36	Galway . .	Kilconnell .	Kilconnell . .	Ballinasloe .	Kilconnell . .	IV.	57
107	Abbeygormacan . .	94	1	18	Galway . .	Longford . .	Abbeygormacan	Ballinasloe .	Abbeygormacan .	IV.	81
23	Abbeygrey or Monasternalea . . .	803	1	14	Galway . .	Killian . .	Athleague . .	Mount Bellew .	Killeroran . .	IV.	66
23	Abbeygrey or Monasternalea . . .	157	3	37	Galway . .	Killian . .	Killeroran . .	Mount Bellew .	Killeroran . .	IV.	67
20	Abbeygrove . .	59	0	26	Kilkenny . .	Gowran . .	Blanchvilleskill	Kilkenny . .	Dunbell . .	I.	327
79	Abbeyhalfquarter, pt.of(b)	93	2	1	Sligo . .	Tireragh . .	Kilmoremoy .	Ballina . .	Ardnaree South .	IV.	557
107	Abbey Island . .	17	1	33	Donegal . .	Tirhugh . .	Kilbarron . .	Ballyshannon	Ballyshannon .	III.	412
106	*Abbey Island* . .	83	1	23	Kerry . .	Dunkerron South	Kilcrohane .	Cahersiveen .	Derrynane .	II.	440
20	Abbey Land . . (c).	—			Cavan . .	Loughtee Upper	Urney . .	Cavan . .	Cavan . .	III.	265
14	Abbeyland . .	68	3	19	Kildare . .	Clane . .	Clane . .	Naas . .	Clane . .	I.	219
40	Abbeyland . .	144	1	8	Kildare . .	Kilkea and Moone .	Castledermot .	Athy . .	Castledermot .	I.	225
15, 20	Abbey Land . .	9	0	11	Longford . .	Ardagh . .	Mostrim . .	Granard . .	Edgeworthstown .	I.	519
17	Abbeyland . .	92	2	23	Meath . .	Duleek Lower .	Duleek . .	Drogheda . .	Duleek . .	I.	668
23	Abbeyland, part of (d)	303	1	25	Meath . .	Navan Lower .	Navan . .	Navan . .	Navan . .	I.	692
6, 7	Abbeyland . .	75	1	25	Westmeath . .	Corkaree . .	Multyfarnham .	Mullingar .	Multyfarnham .	I	874
11	Abbeyland & Charlestown or Ballyeamonaster .	230	1	6	Westmeath . .	Moygoish . .	Kilbixy . .	Mullingar .	Kilbixy . .	I.	893
100, 106	Abbeyland Great . .	812	1	6	} Galway . .	Longford . .	Clonfert . .	Ballinasloe .	Clonfert . .	IV.	82
101	Abbeyland Little .	231	2	5							
17	Abbeyland North . .	26	0	8	Galway . .	Dunmore .	Dunmore . .	Tuam . .	Dunmore . .	IV.	53
112	Abbey-lands, part of (e)	6	0	29	Cork, E.R. . .	Kinsale . .	Kinsale . .	Kinsale . .	Kinsale . .	II.	201
111, 112	Abbey-lands, part of (e).	102	3	1	Cork, E.R. . .	Kinsale . .	Ringcurran . .	Kinsale . .	Kinsale . .	II.	201
107	Abbeylands . .	183	0	18	Donegal . .	Tirhugh . .	Kilbarron . .	Ballyshannon	Ballyshannon .	III.	412
55	Abbeylands . .	171	0	29	Kerry . .	Trughanacmy .	Kilcolman .	Killarney .	Killarney . .	II.	472
79	Abbeylands . . (f)	—			Limerick . .	Connello Lower .	Rathkeale .	Rathkeale .	Rathkeale . .	II.	569
22	Abbeylands . .	40	1	30	Mayo . .	Tirawley . .	Killala . .	Killala . .	Killala . .	IV.	351
9, 10	Abbeylands, part of (g)	200	1	11	Galway . .	Kilcullibeen .	Kilcullibeen .	Waterford .	Waterford . .	II.	899
40, 45	Abbeylands . .	116	2	34	Wicklow . .	Arklow . .	Arklow . .	Rathdrum .	Arklow . .	I.	1095
23	Abbeyland South . .	22	3	14	Galway . .	Dunmore . .	Dunmore . .	Tuam . .	Dunmore . .	IV.	53
25	Abbeyland South,pt.of(d)	22	1	29	Meath . .	Navan Lower .	Navan . .	Navan . .	Navan . .	I.	692
11	Abbeylara . .	296	0	12	} Longford . .	Granard . .	Abbeylara . .	Granard . .	Abbeylara . .	I.	520
11	ABBEYLARA T. . .										
23, 29	Abbeyleix Demesne .	1,321	3	14	Queen's . .	Cullenagh . .	Abbeyleix . .	Abbeyleix .	Abbeyleix . .	I.	792
23	ABBEYLEIX T. . .	—			Queen's . .	Cullenagh . .	Abbeyleix . .	Abbeyleix .	Abbeyleix . .	I.	793
112, 136	Abbeymahon . .	526	0	21	Cork, W.R. . .	Ibane and Barryroe .	Abbeymahon .	Clonakilty .	Abbeymahon .	II.	249
13	Abbey Park . .	16	3	3	Armagh . .	Armagh . .	Armagh . .	Armagh . .	Armagh . .	III.	179
88, 100	Abbeypark . .	283	3	12	Galway . .	Clonmacnowen .	Cloutuskert .	Ballinasloe .	Clontuskert .	IV.	42
92, 103	Abbeyquarter . .	193	1	6	Mayo . .	Costello . .	Annagh . .	Claremorris .	Ballyhaunis .	IV.	311
14	Abbeyquarter North (h)				} Sligo . .	Carbury . .	St. John's . .	Sligo . .	Sligo . .	IV.	542
14	Abbeyquarter South (h)										
3, 24, 27	Abbeyshrule . .	769	1	29	} Longford . .	Shrule . .	Abbeyshrule .	Ballymahon .	Agharra . .	I.	534
23	ABBEYSHRULE T. . .										
31	Abbeyside . . (i)	—			Waterford . .	Decies without-Drum	Dungarvan .	Dungarvan .	Dungarvan . .	II.	885
141	Abbeystrowry . .	428	0	17	Cork, W.R. . .	Carbery West (E.D.)	Abbeystrowry .	Skibbereen .	Skibbereen . .	II.	234
47	Abbeytown . .	263	1	30	Galway . .	Clare . .	Donaghpatrick .	Tuam . .	Donaghpatrick .	IV.	36
29, 36	Abbeytown . .	124	2	22	Mayo . .	Tirawley . 6 .	Crossmolina .	Ballina . .	Crossmolina North	IV.	345

(a) Included in the township of Longford.
(b) The remainder is in the township of Ballina.
(c) Included in the township of Cavan.

(d) The remainder is in the township of Navan.
(e) The remainder is in the township of Kinsale.
(f) Included in the township of Rathkeale.

(g) The remainder is in the city of Waterford.
(h) Included in municipal town of Sligo.
(i) Included in the township of Dungarvan.

B

Fig. 1.4. A page from the 1871 *Townland Index*.

This volume lists alphabetically towns, parishes, baronies and counties that existed in Ireland just prior to its publication in 1837. Whilst not as essential as the *Townland Index* already described, it provides further information about localities. Each entry includes the historical background to an area with information on notable families, landowners and gentry. Alternative spellings for place names are also given which may assist in tracing place names in the *Townland Index*. *The Topographical Dictionary* will be found in the National Archives (NA) and National Library of Ireland (NLI), Dublin, the Public Record Office of Northern Ireland (PRONI), Belfast and libraries around Ireland. It will also be found in the British Library (BL) and Irish Genealogical Research Society (IGRS) in London, and other sources around the world.

Change of place names

During research, you will discover two counties which apparently no longer exist: King's County and Queen's County. In fact, all that has happened is their names have changed. Established during the 16th century in honour of King Phillip II of Spain and his wife Queen Mary, the two counties became, in 1922, Offaly and Laois, respectively, the latter also being known as Leix. Other place names have changed; for example, Cobh in County Cork changed its name to Queenstown in 1849 to commemorate a visit by Queen Victoria, reverting back to Cobh in 1922. It is important to know this sort of thing happened in the past; it may account for the lost place names you were searching for.

Further confusion

Knowledge about the partition of Ireland is also useful. From December 1922, an Act of Parliament enabled two separate governments to exist in Ireland:

(1) an Irish government in Dublin administered 26 counties, including three counties in the Province of Ulster: Cavan, Donegal and Monaghan (see Figs. 1.1 and 1.2). The 26 counties were collectively known as the 'Irish Free State'. In 1937, they became 'Eire' and from 1949 the 'Republic of Ireland'.

(2) a self-governing body in Belfast enabled Britain to retain control of the remaining six counties in Ulster: Antrim, Armagh, Down, Fermanagh, Londonderry and Tyrone. Known as the 'six counties' or 'Northern Ireland', they are also referred to as 'Ulster' when, in fact, the province of Ulster still comprises the nine counties shown in Fig. 1.2.

Pre-1922 records

Where pre-1922 records are categorised according to their province, researchers should note that material relating to Cavan, Donegal and Monaghan will found in the province of Ulster.

The next stage: family footsteps

What should you do next? The next stage is to ascertain from where your ancestor(s) came, and it may be appropriate to mention some of the ground rules applicable to all genealogical research.

Researching backwards

You should try to discover as much as possible about your ancestors, working backwards through your parents, grandparents, etc. It is customary, although not absolutely necessary to trace the male line (tracing the female line can be rewarding too) back through your father, grandfather and so on. Certificates can be very important at this stage. The birth certificate of your grandfather, for example, would normally show the residence of his parents (your great grandparents) and reference to contemporary census documents may reveal their age and place of birth. Elsewhere, census records may be the initial and only clue that ancestors originated in Ireland so it is important at the outset to obtain as much information as possible.

Interviewing parents

To begin, you must talk to your parents and obtain as much information as possible. They may even have commenced research into the family history and possess relevant documentation.

Aunts and uncles

Discuss your research with other relatives; they may have additional information and talk about, matters your parents were unwilling to discuss.

Cousins

Do not neglect cousins. Although usually of the same generation as yourself, they may nevertheless have valuable information.

The family tree

As you progress, it is useful to compile a 'family tree' for keeping a visual check on various stages of your research. Excellent publications describing this procedure have been produced by genealogical and family history organisations worldwide.

Researching sideways

Sideways research, branching into the lives of your ancestors, will add colour and zest, revealing personal information about the way they lived and worked.

Photographs

Always enquire whether photographs exist of the family. In addition to the usual pictures, they may show, on the reverse side, names, dates and places. Photographs will also stimulate conversation with elderly relatives.

Chapter 2

POSTAL RESEARCH

Correspondence

Irish descendants living overseas face particular problems. Many of them believe that ancestral research is impossible or so difficult that it should not be attempted, the problems of distance and available time compounding the situation. In most cases, their only method of conducting research is by mail, and it is this aspect in particular which causes many of the difficulties experienced today.

The initial problems are basic and can be rectified without too much difficulty. Sometimes letters to Ireland are mis-addressed revealing, perhaps mistakenly, the writer's ignorance of Ireland's geography; a case in point being the letter sent to an address in "Dublin, Northern Ireland". Amusing perhaps, but sufficient to cause difficulties for the Irish postal service, resulting in non-delivery of mail and months of anxiety for the sender.

On other occasions, letters reveal the writer's lack of knowledge and consequent ability to state requirements clearly. The resulting frustration for archivists, whose duties may not include letter writing, and professional researchers, cannot be overstated.

The first contact

The discovery of someone who has information about your ancestor is undoubtedly a pleasant surprise, but there will be difficulties; either they live in Ireland, miles from anywhere, or on the other side of the world, leaving you with the problem of how to contact them. The answer, provided you know their address, is to send a letter of enquiry, but before doing this, a few dos and don'ts may be appropriate:

(a) do type/neatly print your letter (see Handwriting, below),
(b) do keep it brief and to the point, and
(c) do enclose a stamped addressed envelope (SAE/SASE) (see The fourth rule, below)
At this stage:
(a) do not write letters of more than one page in length,
(b) do not go into too much detail about your ancestry,
(c) do not supply a bewildering list of names hoping some of them will be recognised, and
(d) do not enclose documents, family trees, histories etc., unless requested.

Once the letter has been composed, the next problem comes to mind and it is one that requires considerable thought; how to obtain a reply to your letter of enquiry. For those conducting postal research, this is arguably the biggest problem they have to contend with and whilst it affects all genealogical research, for some reason Irish research is particularly prone to it. To quote Maeve Catford of Guildford, Surrey, "You hear that, if you write to somebody in Ireland, you won't even get a reply, and that the only thing to do is to go over there."

Hints for genenealogical correspondence

For convenience, correspondence may be categorised according to its destination, as private (to relatives and others who may possess useful information) or official (to archives, libraries, registrars, etc.).

Private
The letter of enquiry
Your first letter, being introductory, must be short and to the point. If you mention your quest, do so briefly; the reply, or lack of it, will indicate whether it is worthwhile pursuing enquiries. A word of caution: the subject of family history should be approached tactfully as the recipient may be nervous about questions concerning the family. Their reply or lack of response may indicate whether further contact is desirable.

Elderly folk
It is a genealogical 'fact of life' that many of your correspondents will be elderly people suffering from the infirmities of old age, arthritis, short-sightedness, etc. and this may affect their response to your letters. This is an important factor and one often contributing to the difficulties of Irish research.

Handwriting
It is easy to assume that, because you can read your own handwriting, everyone else can, so before sending your letter, think of the person to whom you are writing. Will he/she be able to read it? Typed or neatly printed letters are more likely to encourage replies, particularly from those who are incapacitated.

The second rule
The second rule (the first rule will be found in Chapter 1) is to assume that, unless you already know otherwise, the recipient to be elderly, thus reminding you to compile letters with extra care.

Official
When writing to 'official' sources, the foregoing rules about clarity must be adhered to and letters of enquiry should be accompanied by a stamped addressed envelope (see the fourth rule, below), an exception being when fees for services, i.e. photocopying, include the cost of postage. In most cases, archive staff will do their best to satisfy enquirers' needs, but with the best intentions in the world, how can any archivist deal with:

"My ancestor came from Tipperary ... he lived in a cabin ... can you find him for me ...?"

"I don't know where he came from but he was Irish ..."

"I found him in the (English) census records ... which said he was "b. in I." Can you help?"

"My grandfather told me that his father ... here is his photograph ... and then he went to England ... and then he returned ... I enclose a family tree which may help you ..."

Such enquiries are not confined to Irish research. In 1988, Marion Brackpool, then secretary of the East Surrey Family History Society in England, wrote in their journal:

The bulk of our mail ... are the enquiries. They arrive from all corners of the world and can range from membership applications, through straightforward genealogy, to the downright impossible.

Quoting from her mailbag, she referred to two letters from America. The first, in which the writer asked: "Can you tell me anything about my ancestor who was born in England?" but failed to mention the ancestor's name, and the second: "I have enclosed a list of 32 names, can you tell me anything about these people?". But the letter from India took some beating: "I would like a photograph of my grandmother who came from Wandsworth". Marion stressed that none of these letters included any further information. It is clear that the wording of correspondence leaves much to be desired, and may be the cause of many letters remaining unanswered. Ettie Pullman Dip.F.H.S., a noted Australian genealogist, recognises the problem: ". . .the necessity to express one's requests in a clear and concise manner cannot be over-stressed. It really is of the utmost importance."

Much thought should be given to letters of enquiry because your own efforts, in some cases spanning many years, will have led to this moment; it would be a shame to spoil it all by unnecessary haste. A knowledge of the basic principles (Chapter 1), Irish records (Chapter 6), and an analysis of your relatives' statements will help you to determine which records need to be searched, where to address your enquiries, and what to say.

The third rule
A third rule therefore, is to cut out 'waffle' by doing preliminary 'homework' as described in Chapter 1, and drafting your letters, perhaps a number of times, before printing or typing them.

Politeness and civility
Politely worded letters will overcome many difficulties and increase the likelihood of a positive response. Phrases such as "I would be grateful . . ." or "It would be appreciated . . ." are more productive than brash demands like "I want you to find out . . ." or "Look in your records for . . . I'm told you have them". Most people like to create a good impression, but when finishing your letter, avoid the 19th century "I remain your most humble . . ." etc. or the modern version, "I remain Sir, your obedient . . ." etc. In other words, do not humble yourself but phrase your letters in a courteous and business-like manner.

International reply coupons
When writing to Ireland (or anywhere else for that matter), it is common practice to enclose international reply coupons (IRCs) as payment for the return postage and in many cases this has been successful in eliciting replies. This method is particularly convenient when writing to archives and official organisations or contacting professional researchers. In fact, advertisements relating to genealogical services often request the inclusion of IRCs. It is the author's opinion, however, that IRCs have contributed to the problems of Irish research. The reasons are that, in addition to their exhorbitant cost, they can only be exchanged for stamps at a post office (an inconvenient procedure for some recipients) and therefore add to the problems already confronting elderly and handicapped people (see Elderly folk, above). There is also a possibility that in the future some post offices in Ireland may close, thereby increasing difficulties for those living in country areas.

The fourth rule
When writing to someone from whom you expect a reply, always include a stamped and addressed envelope (SAE) or SASE as it is known in some other countries. It is also helpful to include notepaper or space at the bottom of your letter for their reply. (See How to obtain Irish stamps, below.)

Which stamps shall I enclose?
It is not uncommon for family historians overseas to enclose their own country's stamps upon the SAEs they hope will be returned from Ireland and months may pass waiting for the

mail that never appears. Many such cases are due to carelessness and a few guidelines may be appropriate. If you reside in the United Kingdom, you should ascertain, prior to contacting Irish sources, whether to enclose English or Irish stamps. The rule of thumb is simple. Letters returned from the Republic of Ireland require Irish stamps and those from Northern Ireland, because it is part of the United Kingdom, require British stamps. The same rule applies when corresponding from other countries; letters returned from the Republic of Ireland require Irish stamps and those from Northern Ireland require British stamps. Figure 2.1 will assist you to determine the correct return postage from Ireland.

IRISH STAMPS		BRITISH STAMPS
Carlow	Longford	Antrim
Cavan	Louth	Armagh
Clare	Mayo	Down
Cork	Meath	Fermanagh
Donegal	Monaghan	Londonderry
Dublin	Offaly	Tyrone
Galway	Roscommon	
Kerry	Sligo	
Kildare	Tipperary	
Kilkenny	Waterford	
Leitrim	Westmeath	
Leix	Wexford	
Limerick	Wicklow	

Fig. 2.1. 'Postage map' of Ireland.

How to obtain Irish stamps

There is little difficulty purchasing Irish stamps if you live in Ireland, but how can you obtain them if you reside in Britain, or other parts of the world? Irish stamps can be obtained in a number of ways:

(a) Send a request (with money but do not ask for change) to relatives living in Ireland,

(b) request a friend or neighbour who is visiting Ireland to get some for you,

(c) send a request to the Irish Philatelic Society, GPO, Dublin 1, Eire enclosing the appropriate payment, or

(d) if you visit Ireland, purchase some from a post office.

A cheque or banknote is not unreasonable in these circumstances and will be converted according to the current rate of exchange. Any money outstanding could be donated to a charity of the recipient's choice.

Correspondence by e-mail

Many family historians now conduct their correspondence by e-mail (electronic mail) and via the Internet. Further information about these systems will be found in Chap. 7.

Professional research

For many people, particularly those residing overseas, the pressures of work and family commitments do not allow time for research and they may find it expedient to hire someone in Ireland to do the job for them; the question is, who do they contact and, assuming their own knowledge is limited, what do they say? The subject of professional research is a complex one, prompting much discussion about quality of work, reliability, and fees. It cannot be discussed in depth here but the following information may be useful.

Advertisements

Advertisements offering services in the field of Irish research appear regularly in genealogical publications. Unfortunately, a few advertisers have brought the genealogical profession into disrepute, thereby contributing in no small way to the frustrations and problems of Irish research. Enquirers are advised to satisfy themselves as to the researcher's qualifications, work involved and likely fees before committing themselves or parting with money, a procedure that genuine researchers will not object to. The Association of Professional Genealogists in Ireland (APGI), will supply, upon receipt of an SAE/IRC, a list of professional researchers who have proved their ability to do work on behalf of clients and who are bound by a strict code of practice. APGI will investigate all complaints concerning their members. Correspondents are not entirely faultless and when contacting professional researchers may themselves be responsible for some of the problems experienced. Paul Gorry, an experienced genealogist and former secretary of APGI from 1988 to 1991, receives letters from all over the world. Commenting on the content of some of these, he says:

". . . .the major error that most people make is in relation to the way they present their information. They usually fail to differentiate between documented facts and untested family lore, or their own guesswork."

Occasionally, clients fail to notify him of work already done:

"It becomes especially confusing when they have already had work done by another genealogist and . . . refrain from supplying a copy of the report."

"If their entire search is based on theories or their own interpretation of another genealogist's findings, a whole family history could be built on shaky ground".

Another organisation in Ireland, the Association of Ulster Genealogists and Record Agents (AUGRA), also provides a list of researchers who undertake research on a fee-paying basis. Its Secretary, Joan Phillipson, explains why family historians may need professional advice:

"Research in Ireland can be more time consuming than research in England due to records being stored in various locations throughout Ireland. Many records have also been lost."
She adds:

". . . it is sometimes difficult to understand the unavailability of some records, particularly census records, the majority of which (were) destroyed . . . We have a constitution which describes the aims and objectives of the Association and which incorporates procedures to be followed if a complaint is received. However, complaints are virtually nil and we feel this is due to the professionalism of our researchers."

Irish descendants may also need help in tracing ancestors who emigrated from Ireland and comparable organisations exist in other countries for the benefit of family historians. In England, for example, the Association of Genealogists and Record Agents (AGRA) has compiled a strict Code of Practice to which new members agree to adhere, and will supply a copy of its List of Members, including the code of practice, on receipt of £2.50 (UK) or 6 IRCs (overseas). The address of the secretaries will be found in Appendix B. The list indicates the geographical areas and specialist work of individual members, enabling the selection of those whose skills are particularly suited to the research required. A few members work in Ireland and specialise in Irish research.

Dr. Stephen Taylor, currently chairman of AGRA, recognised the difficulties facing prospective clients and offers the following advice:

(a) when responding to advertisements, the most recent should be used to ensure that letters reach their correct destination;

(b) when writing to researchers, enquirers should put their address on the rear of the envelope so that, if it is undelivered for some reason it can be quickly returned; and

(c) having selected a researcher: (i) establish terms first, (ii) write or print requirements clearly, in presentable form; do not send copious pages of information, (iii) when requested, show clearly information already obtained, together with names, addresses and dates, (iv) to avoid duplication, detail clearly the research already carried out, and (v) never send original documents, only copies; important material has sometimes been lost in this way through no fault of the researcher

Please note: It is necessary for those employing professional searchers to keep a file containing (a) copies of all letters sent and (b) all correspondence and enclosures received from researchers.

Not only is this important for following the progress of research, but also replacing losses that may occur in the mail. Such copies will also be useful if disagreements arise (for which a complaints procedure has been drawn up). However, genealogists and record agents are only accepted into AGRA membership after their work has been examined and found satisfactory by the Council of AGRA or the Institute of Heraldic and Genealogical Studies. Suitable references must also be supplied.

Great expectations

Despite encouraging developments in Ireland, much remains to be done. Problems have arisen over the staffing and funding of research centres and many archives are inundated with enquiries from around the world. Enquirers should be prepared for delays and not expect research work to be carried out unless specific arrangements have already been made. (See also Appendix A.)

Bibliography

Alphabetical Index to the Townlands and Towns of Ireland 1871, British Parliamentary Papers HC 1877 XVI.

Beckett, J.C, *The Making of Modern Ireland 1603–1923* Faber and Faber, London, reprinted 1989.

Lewis, Samuel, *Topographical Dictionary of Ireland,* London, 1837.

The General Alphabetical Index to the Townlands and Towns, Parishes and Baronies of Ireland, Alexander Thom, Dublin, 1861, reprinted 1984 by Genealogical Publishing Co. Inc., Baltimore, Massachusetts, USA.

Chapter 3

EXODUS

Part 1: Britain and North America

Introduction

Due to the immigrations of earlier years, Irish descendants overseas may need to conduct research in their own country of residence to discover information about their ancestors' origins in Ireland (see Chapter 1). Australians with convict ancestors are fortunate in this regard because of the quantity and location of material available to them, but a lot of work must still be done to obtain the required information. Enquiries may be hampered by the fact that not all immigrants remained where they landed; thousands who entered Britain during the 19th century for example, wandered around the country looking for work. Similar movement occurred in Canada when thousands of Irish crossed the border, entering the industrial towns and cities of the United States, many of them choosing to go west, track-laying for the railroads or becoming miners and soldiers. In many instances, the trail will lead back not to Ireland but England, to where most emigrants came prior to travelling further afield. The possibilities of an 'English' connection therefore should not be ignored just because Ireland is paramount to your search. Falling into this trap may present you with that for which Irish research is famous, the genealogical paradox (see Fig. 3.1) creating for the unwary researcher even more confusion. This chapter is a summary of Irish emigration. It is not a pretty story but it explains some of the difficulties facing today's researchers and should therefore be told. It will also stimulate your thoughts about the existence of Irish-related material elsewhere, giving you a clearer conception of what is available outside Ireland.

Centuries of emigration

Over the centuries, Ireland succumbed to the emigration of its people and many of them left for political or economic reasons. Approximately 100,000 men, women and children were transported to the North American colonies by Cromwell and, as a result of the Cromwellian and Williamite wars, thousands of Irish soldiers fled to Europe and served with the armies of the continent. During the 17th and 18th centuries, many emigrants to North America were indentured servants who had obtained free passage in return for a period of service with a 'master'. Cruelty and other difficulties, however, caused many of them to abscond, and reward notices requesting information about them often appeared in colonial newspapers of the day. A large number of emigrants were Presbyterian farmers from Ulster who, possessing the necessary skills and capital, were intent upon building a new life. Others were persuaded by earlier settlers to come to the "land that was happy and prosperous". During this period, a number of children were 'kidnapped' by merchants to be sold as servants in the colonies. The end of the Napoleonic wars heralded a flood of Irish Catholic emigrants and from 1820 to 1840, over 226,000 entered the United States.

The American revolution

It was inevitable that immigrants would become involved in the War of Independence,

NAMES OF UNIONS.	NAMES OF PAUPERS.	Age.	WHERE BORN. England and Wales.	Scotland.
		Yrs.		
Ballymahon	Edward Gordon	12	England.	
	William Gordon	11	Ditto.	
	James Cunningham	13	Ditto.	
	Thomas Cunningham	10	Ditto.	
	Mary Keenan	8	Ditto.	
Ballymena	Richard M'Donnell	12		Scotland.
	Mary Davison	12		Ditto.
	Nanny Gillan	14		Ditto.
	William M'Parson	79		Ditto.
Ballymoney	Rose Gauet	2		Scotland.
	John Lewes	4		Ditto.
	Eliza Lewes	2		Ditto.
	Anne Magee	13		Ditto.
Ballyshannon	- - - Nil.			
Ballyvaghan	- - - Nil.			
Balrothery	Ellen Whelan	17	Manchester.	
	Mary Whelan	15	Ditto.	
	Anne Whelan	10	Ditto.	
	James Whelan	9	Ditto.	
	John Whelan	6	Ditto.	
	Patrick Whelan	3	Calderbrooke, near Rochdale.	
	Margaret Whelan	1	Ditto.	
Baltinglass	- - - Nil.			
Banbridge	Anne Campbell	74	Sevenoaks, Kent.	
	Alexander Burr	7		Ayrshire.
Bandon	Margaret Donovan	14	Wales.	
	Catherine Donovan	12	Ditto.	
	John Donovan	10	Ditto.	
	James Lucey	5	England.	
	Thomas Lucey	1¾	Ditto.	
Bantry	Mary Shea	12	London.	
Bawnboy	Alexander Cafferty	11	St. Helen's, England.	
Belfast	John Livingstone	64		Renfrewshire.
	Fanny Johnston	22		Edinburgh.
	Matilda Gribbon	20		Glasgow.
	Daniel Cunningham	48		Renfrewshire.
	Agnes M'Kearnon	33		Dumfrieshire.
	Francis Weir	28		Glasgow.
	Mary Scullion	5 ms.		Ayr.
	Ellen Ramsay	10		Scotland.
	William John Hillis	13		Ayr.
	John Boyle	8		Glasgow.
	William Campbell	9		Dumbarton.
	Mary Campbell	7		Ditto.
	James O'Hara	8		Scotland.
	William Hynds	13		Ditto.
	Jemima Boyle	10		Glasgow.
	Jane Hawkshaw	43	Exeter.	
	John Dickson	77	Westminster.	
	Francis Wherry	67	Newcastle.	
	Elizabeth Smith	7	Whitehaven.	
	Patrick Smith	3	Ditto.	
	Anne Gibbons	9	North Shields.	
	Bernard Davy	40	Liverpool.	
	William Chaney	15	Chester.	
	Francis Keenan	15	Woolwich.	
	Henry Kerr	11	Newcastle-on-Tyne.	
	James Gilmore	9	Liverpool.	
	Patrick Downey	9¼	Manchester.	
	Hugh Gibbons	14	North Shields.	
	John James Paine	10	Liverpool.	
	Edward Dallagher	10	London.	
	George Burkly	9	England.	
	William John Moore	12	Ditto.	
	James Lucas	13	Ditto.	

Fig. 3.1. An Irish genealogical paradox.

15

fighting against the British Army on American soil, and George Washington, recognising their contribution, authorised the password Saint Patrick during one of his campaigns. When the declaration of Independence was signed in 1776, three of its signatories were Irish-born, and some of the others were of Irish descent. Even the printer who produced the first copy was Irish.

The 1790 census

In 1790, the first American census showed that, out of a population of 3,000,000 people, 44,000 were Irish-born and 150,000 claimed Irish descent, figures since disputed by historians who claimed there were many Irish in the country who were unrecorded.

The timber trade and emigration

Because of events in Europe, England by 1807 was relying heavily on imports of Canadian timber, a factor that was to have a profound impact upon Irish emigration.

Around this time, conditions in Ireland were so bad that, for many people, emigration was the only answer. Consequently, masters of empty timber ships returning to Canada realised they could embark fare-paying passengers from Irish ports. These ships were totally unsuitable for this purpose but any improvements increased the fares which, up to now had cost £2–£3 for passage to Quebec. It was not long before shipping companies and merchants took advantage of this new trade, supplying a variety of vessels, many of them little better than rotting hulks, and later nicknamed 'coffin ships' during the famine era. At this time, passengers were unaware how long their journey would take, voyages to New York taking from four to six weeks. Initially, passengers had to supply their own food and were sometimes misled as to the duration of the voyage; upon running out of supplies they had little choice but to purchase more from the Captain's unusually large stocks. Dates of sailings were uncertain, and emigrants frequently ran out of food whilst awaiting embarkation. Voyages across the Atlantic were highly dangerous, particularly in bad weather, and sailings were generally confined to the summer season. Nevertheless, thousands died from shipwreck, accidents, fever and malnutrition.

The cost of passage to New York was high, until immigrants discovered they could travel more cheaply to Canada, subsequently crossing the border into the United States where there was more work and higher wages. But the Irish were not welcome. Despised by Americans and other immigrants, they were considered unhuman, ridden with disease and were frequently attacked. Many were refused jobs because they were Irish.

The English attraction

In spite of historical events, England was a land of opportunity for those who flocked across the Irish sea looking for work. By the 1830s, there were sailings to Liverpool from Dublin, Youghal, Sligo, Waterford and Belfast; hazardous journeys which took, in those early days of sail, anything up to 30 hours to complete. Other events influenced this migration. Irish landlords, anxious to rid themselves of tenants who were holding up land development, evicted them and, in some instances, paid their passage out of the country. Some tenants, using their savings or what they could borrow from friends, travelled to Liverpool where, unable to afford their passage across the Atlantic, they remained. Another factor encouraging immigration was the English Poor Law which entitled all paupers to food or outdoor relief without having to enter a workhouse, thus providing a powerful incentive to leave Ireland. As immigration increased, Irish and English parishes were encouraged by Government to offer passage money as an alternative to supporting the poor.

The Great Famine, 1845–1849

In Ireland, there were many failures of the potato crop (at least 20 since 1728) each one being followed by famine and increased emigration, later fuelled by debt-ridden landlords evicting their tenants. But none was as severe as that which struck in 1845. Beginning in the United States, from where the potato had originated, the blight spread to Europe, England and then Ireland, where the effects were worsened by three weeks of severe wet weather. This, in a country almost totally reliant upon potatoes, heralded a disaster of immense proportions. As conditions worsened (the average life expectancy was only 19 years), roads leading to Irish ports were flooded by thousands of men, women and children striving to reach England for work and food. They entered England mainly through the ports of Liverpool, Glasgow, Swansea, Cardiff and Newport. Liverpool was the main point of entry, and was soon heavily populated by the stream of immigrants arriving daily. In a single day in 1847, 23,866 immigrants received food, and later that same year, during a period of five months, Liverpool was swamped by 300,000 Irish paupers. Inevitably fever struck, and very soon 2,500 people were recorded as having died. Large numbers of immigrants moved on, travelling to other cities and towns in England. In Manchester, the Registrar reported that the Irish were ". . . rambling about the streets in droves" and by December 1846, Glasgow was swamped by 26,335 Irish paupers begging for money and food. They took up residence wherever they could, and at 95, Bridegate, Glasgow, a cellar measuring 10 feet square was found to contain 8 adults and 17 children. Spreading to other Scottish cities, the Irish tended to concentrate in specific places; an example being the Grassmarket, Cowgate and West Port areas of Edinburgh. People resented this 'invasion', particularly where the Irish competed for local jobs, their willingness to accept lower wages resulting in anti-Catholic-Irish riots that were often reported by the newspapers. In England, efforts were made to return those dependent on local relief but the procedures involved were slow and cumbersome. In June 1847, an act of parliament enabled local authorities to return paupers with a minimum of delay despite many of them declaring they would rather die than return. Nevertheless, arrangements went ahead, and orders for summary removal were organised in batches of 80 at a time; many paupers were returned, only to arrive back again later.

As a result of the Passenger Acts, some improvements, financed by increased fares, were made to conditions on board ships but these were inadequate, and failed to prevent passengers being swept overboard in rough seas, or dying of exposure, fever and other causes (see Fig. 3.2). Nor did the Acts prevent unsuitable ships from leaving smaller ports on the west coast of Ireland. So great was the haste to leave, that many sailed during the winter season and were wrecked within sight of the shore.

Quarantine

It has been estimated that, in 1847, 17,000 emigrants died from fever before reaching America, a figure excluding deaths from other causes. 'Famine fever', a combination of typhus and relapsing fever, was feared by crews and passengers alike. Thought by some to have originated in the Liverpool slums where many emigrants had lived, the disease spread wherever they went.

Grosse Isle

In 1832, a quarantine station was established on Grosse Isle, at the mouth of the St. Lawrence River, and it was to here that emigrant ships bound for Canada, hove to (see Fig. 3.2). Infected passengers and crew were detained in a hospital built to accommodate 150 patients, and was swamped with 2,500; the line of ships waiting to be inspected stretched several miles down the St. Lawrence. Whilst giving evidence before a committee of enquiry, a doctor at Grosse Isle stated:

"I have been attached to the station at Grosse Isle for the last six years ... we had last year upwards of 22,000 immigrants, the poorer class of Irish, and the English paupers sent by parishes ..."

But the quarantine procedures were inadequate, and the fever spread, eventually reaching St. John, Quebec and Montreal. Procedures broke down and on 28 October 1847, the hospital on Grosse Isle closed.

Staten Island

A quarantine station had been established outside New York harbour on Staten Island. Vessels wishing to enter New York were inspected and after a brief medical examination, infected passengers and crew were detained in the hospital. Employment on the Island was provided by the quarantine station and some light industry, workers commuting from New York. By 1847, at the height of the famine, an hourly ferry service had been established making it possible for New York residents to visit sick relatives in the hospital. Two days in the week were eventually set aside for these visitors as normal restrictions were ineffective. It was subsequently reported that on those days 'hundreds and thousands' were coming and going in ferry boats. Passengers with money often refused to be quarantined and entire crews of ships that had been detained took transport and disappeared in New York. It was not long before the fever also reached New York. Staten Island had a resident population on the island which had lived there for years in peace and security. The dangers from infection were obvious and residents frequently complained about disgusting rubbish from emigrant ships being washed up on the shore. The smell from the Marine Hospital was carried on the wind towards houses and residents were forced to keep the windows closed all day. Alarmed at this threat to their health and privacy, they attacked the hospital in 1856, and in 1858 burned it down.

Ellis Island

From 1856, immigrants not suffering from fever landed at the former concert hall Castle Garden and from 1892 until 1943, Ellis Island took over as the immigration centre, becoming, in 1963, a national historic site in tribute to American immigrants. In 1990, following a massive restoration, it became a museum dedicated to the earlier immigrants who had arrived from all over the world.

Deer Island

On 8 June 1847, near Boston, another quarantine station had been established on Deer Island where similar procedures were adopted. It closed the following year on 9 February 1848.

No. 3.—Report of Vessels Boarded at the Quarantine Station, Grosse Isle; from 20th day of May, at 3 A.M., to 20th day of May, at 8 P.M., 1841.

Ship and Name	Captain's Name	From	Date of Sailing	Arrival	Cargo	Cabin	Steerage	Consigned to	Date of Release	Remarks
Ship Sea Bunny	Thomas Brympton	Hull	April 1	May 20	General	1	100	Birstall	May 20	Two adults, from consumption, took ill before leaving Hull.
Barque Ursula	Thomas Clark	Cork	14	"	Ballast	:	114	Lemesurier	"	An infant died, and one of the crew lost overboard.
Barque Ninian	Thomas Bowler	Limerick	9	"	"	:	182	Order	"	
Brig Titin	Daniel Rose	Cork	9	"	"	::	132	Price	"	An infant, from debility, died on the voyage.
Barque Typein	Richard Haycock	Cork	11	"	"	1	190	Chapman	"	An infant born and died on board.
Ship Vitain	Thomas Simpson	Falmouth	3	"	"	:	40	Order	"	
Barque Guilford	Isaac Redd	Bristol	3	"	General	1	17	Levy and Co.	"	
Brig James Cook	J. Folin	Limerick	29	"	Ballast	1	161	Order	May 22	
Brig Empress	C. Hodgson	Dublin	16	"	Salt	3	191	"	May 30	Small-pox among these passengers, but no deaths.
Ship Sir G. Prevost	A. Mackay	Newry	11	"	Ballast	1	292	"	"	Two children died on the voyage.
Barque Springhill	M. Hall	Kilula	22	"	Salt	1	229	"	"	
Barque Wellington	Patrick M'Intyre	Belfast	21	"	Salt	1	396	Parke and Co.	May 21	Measles broke out; six children died.
Barque Albion	William Robinson	Londonderry	22	"	Ballast	:	143	Order	May 20	One child died.
Brig Congress	James M'Neill	Belfast	16	"	General	:	213	Greenfields	"	Two children died, and two born on voyage.
Barque Eagle	William Long	Liverpool	15	"	Ballast	:	17	Parker and Co.	"	
Barque Sarah Stewart	Archibald Low	Belfast	5	"	Ballast	:	273	Order	"	
Brig Ann Moore	Robert Paton	Limerick	12	"	"	1	160	"	"	An infant died on the voyage.
Brig Queen Victoria	William Rose	Sligo	22	"	"	:	175	"	"	
Brig Springflower	Joseph Simons	Padstow	17	"	"	:	33	Gilmour	"	
Ship Leader	J. Phelan	Liverpool	15	"	General	5	63	Froste	"	
Barque Robert and George	Peter Dickson	Newcastle	3	"	"	6	22	Budden	"	

No. 4.—Report of Vessels Boarded at the Quarantine Station, Grosse Isle; from 21st day of May to 23rd day of May, 1841.

Ship and Name	Captain's Name	From	Date of Sailing	Arrival	Cargo	Cabin	Steerage	Consigned to	Date of Release	Remarks
Barque Aberdeen	Charles Duggan	Liverpool	April 13	May 20	General	:	46	Froste and Co.	May 21	An infant died on the voyage.
Brig Cornwallis	Henry Dernois	Waterford	19	21	Ballast	:	131	Levy and Co.	"	
Brig Helen Stewart	John Stuart	Westport	20	"	"	:	156	Tibbits	"	
Ship St. Patrick	Alex. Webster	Cork	11	"	"	3	49	Chapman	"	
Barque Industry	Thomas Barrett	Sligo	21	22	"	:	191	Order	May 22	
Barque Tamerlane	George Fisher	Liverpool	5	"	General	:	34	Froste and Co.	"	One of the crew died from apoplexy.
Barque Baltic	William Curdrum	Yarmouth	7	"	Ballast	:	118	Pemberton and Co.	"	
Brig Fairy	James Nicol	Truro	20	"	"	:	42	Price and Co.	"	
Brig Duchess of Buccleugh	John Blair	Dumfries	3	"	"	:	96	"	"	One of these passengers, a female, washed overboard by a sea.
Brig Brianabs	Isaac Ilugill	Limerick	12	23	General	:	117	"	May 23	
Brig Mary Rowe	Joseph Humphries	Baltimore	28	"	Ballast	:		Syme and Co.	"	

Signed) G. W. Douglas, M.D.,
Medical Superintendent.

Fig. 3.2. Extract from British Parliamentary Papers in 1841 referring to Grosse Island, Canada.

19

Postscript

In a valley on Grosse Isle, there are two monuments. On one is written

In this secluded spot lie the mortal remains of 5,294 persons who, flying from pestilence and famine in Ireland in the year 1847, found in America but a grave

and on the other

Sacred to the memory of thousands of Irish immigrants . . . ended here their sorrowful pilgrimage.

The Irish influence

Discrimination was forgotten as the Irish became accepted into American life. Lacking skills, they became an inexhaustible supply of labour and many were employed on road and canal construction from 1815 to 1832. Irish women were employed in laundries or as housemaids and waitresses. Immigration continued unabated, and the Irish took jobs that Americans were reluctant to do. By 1850, over 300 policemen in New York were Irish, resulting in a contemporary view that there were no American policemen in the city, a subject caricatured in publications of the day. Irish traditional music, imported by immigrants, enabled them to retain their 'Irishness' in the various communities. The Chicago police helped keep this aspect of Irish culture alive when one immigrant, Francis O'Neill, Chicago Police Chief from 1901 to 1905, and his sergeant, James Early, visited sessions recording the music of their native land. *O'Neill's Music of Ireland*, first published in 1963, contained hundreds of these tunes, many bearing the names of their composers, or musicians who played them, valuable information for those with musical ancestors. A criticism made against O'Neill was that his force contained an unusually large proportion of Irish musicians!

By 1860, one third of New York's population were Irish-born, the city becoming known as The 'Largest Irish City in the World'. And to the north-east, in Providence, Rhode Island, the 1859 Directory was noted for the number of Kelleys (sic) listed.

During the Civil War, Irish regiments on both sides consisted almost entirely of Irishmen, and after the war, many ex-soldiers and Irish-Americans were engaged in the construction of railroads.

Towards the end of the 19th century, the Irish dominated the fire and police departments of many of the larger cities; particularly New York, Chicago and Boston. The Irish also permeated other occupations. In his book *A Portrait of The Irish in America*, William Griffin wrote

For Italian, Slavic or Jewish immigrants at the turn of the century, their early experience of America often involved . . . Irish customs officers, foremen, municipal clerks, and schoolteachers that left many of them wondering whether there was anyone in the United States but the Irish

From 1820 to 1900, an estimated 3,873,000 Irish emigrated to the United States, 1,700,000 of them due to the Great Famine. By 1870, the total population of the United States numbered 38,558,371 of whom 1,855,827 were Irish-born; half of them residing in the States of New York, Pennsylvania and Massachusetts (see Chapter 4).

At least 1,000,000 people died in Ireland during the famine, but their deaths were never recorded, civil registration not having commenced until 1864 (see Chapter 6).

Part 2: Australia, New Zealand and South Africa

Emigration and transportation to Australia

The early settlers to Australia comprised convicts, soldiers, seamen, and government officials; 'free' settlers did not arrive until a few years later. The story of Australian settlement must therefore include an account of the system of transportation that began to North America and ended in Australia.

Transportation: the beginnings

In England during the middle ages, crime was rampant. The judicial system was inadequate, prisons were overflowing and punishment ineffective. In 1597, Queen Elizabeth I approved an Act of Parliament that was intended to punish "rogues, vagabonds and sturdy beggars". As a result, large numbers of men and women accused of offences were sent to the West Indian colonies. Oliver Cromwell made use of the system when he invaded Ireland and sent thousands of prisoners to the sugar plantations of the West Indies and other colonies.

In an effort to deter crime, and provide a source of cheap labour, a Transportation Act of 1717 provided the system with a legal footing, and by 1777, 30,000 men and women, including 10,000 Irish, had been despatched from the United Kingdom to the colonies of North America.

The 'discovery' of Australia

In 1770, Captain Cook, in charge of an expedition to Tahiti to observe the transit of Venus across the sun, had sighted the east coast of Australia (the Dutch, French and Spanish had already made landings) and 'officially' claimed it for England, an action that was to have a marked effect upon history.

The American War of Independence

On the other side of the world, the North American colonies were becoming difficult, objecting to taxes and other restrictions imposed by the British upon their trade. They rebelled, and in 1776, refused to accept any more prisoners from England. The supply of convicts was halted, temporarily it was thought, until the colonists could be taught a lesson and transportation resumed.

The hulks

Again, English prisons overflowed, and in order to relieve the pressure, an Act of Parliament known as the Hulks Act, was passed. This permitted old rotting ships, some of which could barely float, to be used as floating prisons (hulks) until the American problem was resolved, or a decision made as to where the prisoners could be sent. The Thames and ports on the south coast became dotted with hulks and some were also placed outside Kingstown and Cobh harbours in Ireland. Conditions on board were appalling; there was no recreation and sanitation was virtually non-existent. Many prisoners died, their bodies being sold for medical research and coffins purporting to contain them were often filled with earth and stones.

The First Fleet

The American 'nut' could not be cracked, and it was decided to send the convicts to that new land on the other side of the world, Australia. A base at Botany Bay would be useful for trade with the East Indies and the convicts could be used as labourers for building. The neccesary arrangements were made and in 1786, Arthur Phillip was selected as Captain-General and Governor of the proposed settlement. On 13 May 1787, what became known as the First Fleet, comprising 11 ships and 1,487 passengers of which more than 750 were convicts, sailed from Portsmouth. The 13,000 mile voyage took seven months and on January 20 the following year, the fleet arrived at Botany Bay. The shore was unsuitable for landing and Phillip ordered the fleet north to Port Jackson where they arrived at Sydney Cove on January 26.

Three years later, in June 1790, a Second Fleet arrived but the voyage had not been without tragedy; of approximately 1,000 convicts on board, 267 had died. The arrival of a Third Fleet and 1,864 prisoners revealed that another 199 had perished.

Free Settlers

Being labourers, most convicts lacked other skills required for building, and it was decided to obtain men who were skilled in various crafts. In 1793, the first 'free' settlers arrived.

Transportation from Ireland

In Ireland, prisoners eligible for transportation were despatched to the port of Cobh in County Cork from where in 1791, the first Irish convict ship, *The Queen*, sailed with 159 prisoners on board, arriving in Sydney on September 29. Political unrest and general lawlessness in Ireland led to the government taking drastic measures and certain districts were proclaimed 'disturbed'. This led to many arrests and transportation without trial; by 1798, there were 653 Irish convicts in New South Wales. The flow of prisoners continued and between 1825 and 1835, 9,500 prisoners from the Irish hulks *Essex* and *Surprise* were transported. Between 1837 and 1840, a further 3,000, including 873 women, had been despatched. Eventually, the Irish hulks were closed down and their prisoners transferred ashore. By 1840, transportation from Ireland had ceased.

'Free' emigration

From 1838, as a result of a change in colonial policy, the British Government actively encouraged families to emigrate. The flow of settlers increased and various schemes were introduced, enabling them to obtain 'assisted' passages. Convicts also gained from a scheme allowing some of them to be joined by their spouses, many of whom settled happily in Australia.

As the need for labour grew and more immigrants poured into the country, it became necessary to regulate the quality of arrivals; males were not to exceed 35 years of age and unmarried women 30 years. Immigrants were to be selected from mechanics, farmers, miners, labourers and domestic servants, and unmarried women were allowed 21 days to find suitable employment.

The education of Irish immigrants left much to be desired. A cartoon first appearing in the *Melbourne Punch* on 18 July 1872 and reproduced in *The Irish Australians*, captured the atmosphere. 'Bridget' is being interviewed by a stern-looking prospective employer:

Bridget:	"Shure, ma'am, I knows jography too, we waas taught it coming out."
Mistress:	"Indeed; then do you know how many hemispheres there are?"
Bridget:	"Shure, an there's two, ma'am, Oirland and Australy."

The Irish were not popular. The following are extracts from the diary of a fellow emigrant Henry John Ford and reproduced in *Generation,* the journal of the Genealogical Society of Queensland.

23.12.1862   . . . Proceeding to Ireland where we are to take up a great number of passengers (emigrants).

1.1.1863   . . . anchored at Queenstown Harbour at 12 noon.

2.1.1863   Went on shore and had a good walk through the town . . . the inhabitants appeared to be very dirty and poor.

4.1.1863   We set sail this afternoon and soon lost sight of old Ireland . . . the Irish came on board on Friday to our utter dismay . . . men women and children . . . a number of them barefooted and such noise and confusion I never before heard or witnessed. They jumped over tables and forms and seized several casks of biscuits which they immediaitely broke open and devoured . . . The priest is now on board and that alters the aspects of affairs altogether . . . had I known the number and class of our friends, I certainly should not have been in such a hurry to sail.

19.2.1863   I regret to say two children died today . . . they were sown in canvas and thrown overboard.

20.2.1863   The children are suffering greatly from measles.

22.2.1863   Another little boy thrown overboard from measles.

10.3.1863   The captain gave up his own cabin to the woman who was confined . . . sat up with her all night feeding her with his own hand . . . the poor creature died . . . thrown overboard . . .

12.3.1863   Had an awful night . . . sea poured down the hatchway into the cabins . . . screams and groans of terrified women . . .

17.3.1863   This is St. Patrick's day. The Irish hailed the morning with music and dancing and made a tremendous noise all night.

28.3.1863   We spoke with a steamer this morning from New Zealand bound for Melbourne. One child died and another born today.

30.3.1863   A quarrel took place between some of the Irish passengers and crew, which might have led to serious results but for the interference of the priest.

Orphans

During the latter part of the 1840s, a scheme was set up whereby orphan girls between 14 and 19 years of age were selected from Irish workhouses and shipped to Australia, the purpose being to solve a labour problem on the domestic front and redress an imbalance between sexes in the colony. A government agent, Lt. Henry, visited Irish workhouses selecting suitable orphans. On one occasion, he chose 24 girls from the workhouse at Magherafelt, arranging their journey to Plymouth via Belfast and Dublin, from where they sailed on 17 July 1848.

The scheme was unpopular with Australians, many of the girls being illiterate, Catholic and ... Irish, but it undoubtedly served its purpose, for many of the girls entered domestic service or married and settled down with families. At its conclusion, over 4,000 orphans had been sent to Australia from workhouses in Ireland.

The gold rush

The discovery of gold in 1851 attracted many opportunists from other countries, including Ireland and America, many of whom remained in Australia after the rush had subsided.

Convict landowners

After serving their sentences, some convicts became landowners, offering jobs to others who were seeking employment. As a result of Irish settlement, parts of Australia became 'Irish', an example being an area in New South Wales where it was said that a local priest, Father Lovat, could ride his horse continuously for 300 miles on Irish-held soil.

Transportation was officially abolished in 1852, but continued to Western Australia to fulfil a requirement for cheap labour. By the time it finally ceased in 1868, approximately 162,000 convicts had been sent from the United Kingdom. Of these, 70% were English, 25% Irish, and 5% Scottish. 1,537,400 free settlers also arrived during this period.

Today, an estimated 1,000,000 Australians are descended from convicts. Until recently, such ancestry was considered embarrassing but that has now changed and many Australians are currently engaged in ancestral research (see Chapter 4).

New Zealand

No convicts were sent to New Zealand although there was a steady flow of settlers from the United Kingdom. In 1840, one of these, William Hobson, became the first Irish governor and served in that post for two years. During the 1860s, the discovery of gold attracted speculators from around the world, many of whom settled in the country.

The 1870s saw immigration on a large scale, during which many more Irish entered the country, females for domestic service and indentured labourers to work on the new farms. In 1981, Irish descendants in New Zealand comprised about 14% of the total population.

Existing material

Details of movements and subsequent settlement were often recorded in official documentation, much of which still exists today (see Chapter 4).

South Africa

Many Irish went to South Africa, some as convicts, some to become labourers in the gold mines during the 1880s and 1890s, and some policemen. From 1874 and 1882 when the Natal and Cape Police were formed, respectively, 28% of recruits were Irish. Many were recruited in Ireland and had their fares paid. Recruits born in South Africa of Irish parents were proud to call themselves 'Colonial Irish'. From 1860, a decision was made that men recruited in Ireland were to pay the full cost of their fares and it was from about this period that the flow of Irish lessened. In 1876, a report in the *Cape Town Daily News* stated:

> We are afraid we could not induce the Irish labouring classes to come to this colony in anything like sufficient numbers. They know nothing of it . . . but they know all about America and Australia, or think they do, having heard them talked about from their infancy by those who had friends there.

In all, over 1,000 Irishmen served in the Natal, and Cape Mounted Police. An interesting comment was made by Donal McCracken in *Familia*. Referring to the late 19th century he wrote that ". . . the Irish in the Cape Mounted Police and Natal Mounted Police had been as prominent as the Irish in the New York Police." By 1904, approximately 20,000 Irish-born people were recorded in South Africa, a figure excluding those of Irish descent.

Bibliography

See the end of Chapter 4.

Chapter 4

THE SEARCH BEGINS

Searching for records

Passenger lists

From 1819, the Passenger Acts required masters of foreign ships arriving in the United States to hand lists of passengers to the customs authorities. Not many of these 'Passenger Arrival Lists' have survived, but copies and extracts covering the period 1820–1905 will be found in the National Archives, Washington DC. An Act of 1882 resulted in the compilation of 'Immigration Passenger Lists' (manifests). Those from the period 1883–1945 will also be found in the National Archives, Washington.

Other lists compiled between 1890 and 1960 show names of passengers travelling from the United Kingdom to countries outside Europe. Many of the Irish who travelled via Britain to North America and Canada are included. These 'Outward Passenger Lists' will be found in the Public Record Office, Kew, London.

In 1985, P. William Filby produced three volumes of the *Passenger and Immigration Lists Index* which have since been supplemented, and between 1983 and 1986, Ira Glazier produced seven volumes of *Famine Immigrants: Lists of Irish Immigrants 1846–1851*. The value of such tomes speak for themselves and copies will be found in Archives around the world.

Few records exist concerning voluntary emigrants to Australia and New Zealand before the Outward Passenger Lists commenced in 1890. Some transportation records refer to 'free' emigrants, usually the spouses and families of convicts who travelled under the special schemes.

For researchers in England, details of emigrants and cabin passengers to New Zealand from 1839 to 1850 will be found in the New Zealand Company records in the Public Record Office, Kew, London.

Assisted immigrants

Records of 'assisted' immigrants to New South Wales, including the *Index to Assisted Irish Immigrants to NSW 1840–1870* are held by the State Library, Sydney. These records show, in addition to other information, details of immigrants' parents.

Orphans

Records of orphans travelling to Australia under the special scheme will be found in Australian State archives.

Convict records

Australian State archives hold large quantities of material relating to convicts, and indexes are also available to help researchers. The Genealogical Society of Victoria's Convict Research Centre offer a service to members whereby they can quickly ascertain if a particular name belongs to a convict (see also Chapter 5).

In 1988, to commemorate the Australian Bicentenary, the Irish Government presented Australia with copies of their transportation records listing approximately 40,000 Irish convicts sent to Australia during the period 1788–1868. These are held by the State Library,

Sydney. The originals are stored in the National Archives, Dublin.

The Public Record Office in Kew, London holds Convict Transport Registers for the period 1787–1867 (Ref: HO 11). Also in the PRO will be found New South Wales Original Correspondence (Ref: CO 201) which includes lists of convicts and settlers.

Newspapers

The archives of national and local newspapers can reveal useful information about Irish ancestors. The National Library of Ireland has a large quantity of Irish newspapers and some libraries have collections relating to their county. In England, the British Library's Newspaper Library, London, has a large collection of Irish national and local newspapers. The Newspaper Library holds local and national Irish newspapers from 1700, and a more complete collection from 1869. They also stock a large collection of 19th century newspapers from countries that formed the British Empire.

Irish newspapers frequently carried advertisements showing dates of sailings from Irish ports, often indicating the routes taken by intending emigrants:

ANCHOR LINE

Londonderry to New York (Direct)

Devonia	4270 tons	Friday	20th Aug
Anchoria	4168 tons	Friday	27th Aug
Ethiopia	4004 tons	Friday	3rd Sept
Bolivia	4050 tons	Friday	10th Sept
Circassia	4271 tons	Friday	17th Sept
Devonia	4270 tons	Friday	24th Sept
Anchoria	4168 tons	Friday	1st Oct
Ethiopia	4004 tons	Friday	8th Oct

FARES Saloon, Cabin, Twelve, Fourteen, and sixteen Guineas...

For further particulars apply to
HENDERSON BROTHERS
80, Foyle Street
Londonderry ...

Passengers can obtain tickets from Sligo (via
Enniskillen) to Derry, for 9s 6d each, leaving
Sligo at 8 a.m. on Thursdays by Walsh's car,
they reach Derry at 4 p.m.

REDUCED RAILWAY FARES TO LONDONDERRY AND DUBLIN

Passengers booked for Anchor Line can obtain
through tickets to Londonderry and Dublin, from
the principal stations of the Midland Great
Western Railway at greatly reduced rates.

Sligo Champion, 18 September 1880

Elsewhere in the United Kingdom, disturbances between immigrants and local people were often reported in newspapers; these included the names and addresses of those concerned. Occasionally innocent pastimes got out of hand when alcohol was consumed, such cases frequently ending in court.

HELENSBURGH POLICE COURT

An Irish Row

"......in the afternoon, a number of 'boys' assembled in the house of Barclay O'Donnell in Havelock Place (Helensburgh) for shelter and enjoyment. The depressing influence of the weather had to be counterbalanced, and whisky . . . liberally consumed. The 'boys' got hearty and wanted a dance . . . and Barclay called at the house of a Mrs. Fee who lives below him and induced a lodger of hers, one James Davies, who is a skilful performer on the flute, to join the party upstairs and supply the needed music. After this, the fun seems to have got somewhat furious . . .

About eleven o'clock she made a third visit for the purpose of getting home her lodger, Davis (sic), who had been blowing away at his flute vigorously. . . On Mrs. Fee going up on this last visit it was proposed to give her a dram . . . Davis then wished to take the bottle with him . . . and to this Barclay objected, others took part in the dispute . . . One of the party got hold of the bottle . . . broke it on the hearth, first, however, bringing (it) in contact with somebody's head . . . the noise brought . . . numerous parties . . . one of these, a Rodger Carr, regarding it as a 'free fight' and without waiting to inform himself of the merits of the dispute . . . struck out effectively, he being sober. At this stage the police interfered . . . and on Saturday, the said Michael Gibbons, Barclay O'Donnell, James Davis (sic) and Rodger (sic) Carr were . . . fined 10s for their respective shares in the disturbance."

Dumbarton Herald & County Advertiser, 6th September 1867

In the United States, *The Boston Pilot* published advertisements from residents and immigrants enquiring for information about relatives. *The Quebec Mercury* also printed names of some passengers arriving at Quebec.

Australia's first newspaper, *The Sydney Gazette and New South Wales Advertiser* contained details of ships and passengers, plus birth, marriage and death notices. Copies of the paper covering the period 1803–1842 are available in Archives around New South Wales.

Pre-1876 death and marriage notices in New Zealand newspapers can be informative, particularly as certificates for that period contain little information of use to genealogists. Birth notices were somewhat limited.

Civil registration

Wherever emigrants settled, there were births, marriages and deaths. In England, where civil registration commenced in 1837, local 'events' were recorded by Registrars, who sent copies to the General Registrar now the Family Records Centre (FRC) in London. These included events amongst the immigrant population, provided they were notified to the authorities.

Scottish civil registration commenced in 1855 and marriage certificates of that year displayed a surprising amount of information (Fig. 4.1). This was the only year such details were shown, although subsequent certificates still showed more information than English

No.	When, where, and how married.	Signatures of the Parties.	Residence. Present.	Usual.	Age.	Rank or Profession, and Relationship of Parties (if related).	Condi... If a Widower or Widow, whether Second or Third Marriage.
56	On September Thirtieth 1855 At Dumbarton Marriage (After Banns) was solemnized between us according to the Rites & Ceremonies of the Roman Catholic Church	(Signed) James Davidson His X Mark	Helensburgh	Helensburgh	19	Labourer	Bachelor
		(Signed) Ellen Cryan	Helensburgh	Helensburgh	19	Servant	Spinster

Birthplace, and when and where registered.	Parents' Names.	Rank, Profession, or Occupation.	If a regular Marriage, Signatures of Officiating Minister and Witnesses.	If irregular, date of Extract Sentence of Conviction, or Decree of Declarator, and in what Court pronounced.	When and where registered, and Signature of Registrar.
Born in Sligo Ireland 1836	Edward Davidson & Nelly Davidson Maiden Name O'Connon		(Signed) John McDonald Roman Catholic Clergyman Dumbarton		1855 October 4th At Dumbarton
Born in Sligo Ireland 1836	Stephen Cryan & Winny Cryan Maiden Name Marn		(Signed) John Macdonald Witness (Signed) Jane O'Donnell Witness		(Signed) William Jardine Registrar

Fig. 4.1 1855 Scottish marriage certificate. (Crown copyright.)

29

ones, death certificates for example, showing parents' names. Due to their vastness, America and Canada have no central repositories for storing birth, marriage, and death records, each State (Province in Canada) being responsible for its own 'vital records'. These commenced at different times; the Eastern States and Provinces, because of earlier settlement, commencing registration first.

In Australia, civil registration is similarly organised, each State being responsible for its own records.

In New Zealand, the registration of births and deaths began in 1848 and marriages in 1854. Certificates before 1876 contain little information of use to genealogists but newspaper notices of the time may give further information. (See *Newspapers,* above.)

In South Africa, centralisation of civil registration only began during the present century and research in these records is not permitted. Certificates are issued in return for exact details on the application. Documentation exists for some 19th century government-aided British settler schemes. The names of many notable policemen in South Africa will be found in *Dictionary of South African Biography* and *Men of the Times* .

Census returns

Census returns in the United Kingdom are stored centrally at the Family Records Centre (FRC) a branch of the Public Record Office, London and New Register House, Edinburgh being the respective repositories for England and Scotland. The most useful returns, not confined to statistics, of both countries are those from 1841; the 1851 and successive returns listing 'famine' immigrants who remained in the United Kingdom. Not all immigrants were included, Irish mistrust and enumerators' fear resulting in many omissions.

In North America, a federal (national) census was usually conducted every 10 years from 1790, individual States and counties organising their own censuses on a less regular basis. Many settlers were included in these.

In Australia, few census records survive from the 19th century; they were destroyed after statistical information had been extracted. Information from the 1828 census of NSW, listing over 35,000 people, has survived and the contents have been published by Sainty and Johnson. From 1788, a number of 'musters' were held in New South Wales and Tasmania which, although mainly concerned with convicts, also included some of their families.

Also in Australia, Dr. Richard Reid of the Heraldry and Genealogy Society of Canberra has compiled an index of Irish immigrants arriving in New South Wales during the period 1848–1868. These show, in addition to other details, names of immigrants and their county of origin.

Workhouse Records

Many of the Irish paupers who benefitted from the English Poor Laws will be found in records held by county record offices in England. Fewer records of this nature exist in Ireland but enquirers should contact the NA, PRONI or relevant county library to ascertain availability.

Bibliography to Chapters 3 and 4

Adams, William Forbes, *Ireland and Irish Emigration To The New World,* Genealogical Publishing Co. Inc., Baltimore (1980).

Ancestor, Vol. 18, No. 3, Genealogical Society of Victoria, Australia, 1987.

Bell, Russ, Australian Connection, *Family Tree Magazine,* Vol. 4, No. 3, 1988.

Bell, Russ, The First Settlement in Australia, *Family Tree Magazine,* Vol. 4, No. 7, 1988.

Bellam, Michael, The Irish in New Zealand, *Familia,* Vol. 2, No. 1, Ulster Historical Foundation, Belfast, 1985.

Bevan, Amanda and Duncan, Andrea, *Tracing Your Ancestors in The Public Record Office,* HMSO, London, 4th edn., 1990.

Bradley, Ann Kathleen, *History of The Irish in America,* Chartwell Books, New Jersey, 1986.

Chiswell, Ann V., Convicts Destined for New South Wales, Australia, *Family Tree Magazine,* Vol. 4, No. 3, 1988.

Costello, Con, *Botany Bay,* Mercier Press, Dublin, 1987.

Currer-Briggs, Noel, *Worldwide Family History,* Routledge and Kegan Paul, 1982.

Dear, Robert B., Samuel Speed, the Last Convict in Australia, *Family Tree Magazine,* Vol. 7, No. 11, 1991.

Dictionary of South African Biography, Cape edition, 1906, Transvaal edition, 1905.

Ellis, Peter Beresford, *Hell or Connaught,* Blackstaff Press, Belfast, reprinted, 1989.

Filby, P. William, North American Passenger Lists, *ISBGFH Newsletter,* Vol. 11, No. 3, 1982.

Filby, P. William and Lower, Dorothy M. (ed.), *Passenger and Immigration Lists Index 1992, Supplement: A Guide to Published Arrivals Records of More Than 2,029,000 Passengers Who Came to the New World,* Gale Research, 1992.

Gillen, Mollie, *The Founders of Australia,* Library of Australian History, Sydney, 1989.

Glazier, Ira, *The Famine Immigrants, 1846–51,* Genealogical Publishing Company, Baltimore, 1983.

Griffin, William D., *The Irish in America 550–1972,* Oceana Publications Inc., New York, 1973.

Griffin, William D., *A Portrait of the Irish in America,* Charles Scribner's Sons, New York, 1981.

Guide to Genealogical Research in the National Archives (Canada), National Archives Trust Fund Board, Canada.

Hadden, Gordon William, South African Research, *ISBGFH,* Vol. 11, No. 4, 1989.

Hawkings, D. *Bound For Australia,* Phillimore, Chichester, 1987.

Hickey, D.J and Doherty, J.E., *A Dictionary of Irish History 1800–1980,* Gill and MacMillan, Dublin, reprinted 1989.

Holden, Keith, Aspects of Convict Research and Records, *Ancestor,* Vol. 19, No. 3, 1988.

Hughes, R., *The Fatal Shore,* Pan Books, London, 1987.

James, Alwyn, *Scottish Roots,* MacDonald Publishers, Midlothian, Scotland, reprinted 1988.

Johnson, W. Branch, *The English Prison Hulks,* Phillimore, Chichester, revised edition, 1970.

Kelly, M.J., My Projects, *The New Zealand Genealogist,* Vol. 21, No. 206, 1990.

Kyle, Noeline, *Tracing Family History in Australia,* Methuen, Australia, 1985.

McClaughlin, Trevor, Barefoot and Pregnant? Female Orphans who Emigrated from Irish Workhouses to Australia 1848–50, *Familia,* Vol. 2, No. 3, Ulster Historical Foundation, 1985.

McCracken, Donal P, The Irish in South Africa: The Police, A Case Study, *Familia,* Vol. 2, No. 7, Ulster Genealogical and Historical Guild, 1991.

Maher, Brian, Ireland Over Here. 19th Century Irish Immigrants in Southern New South Wales, *The Irish Australians,* The Society of Australian Genealogists and Ulster Historical Foundation, 1984.

Maitland, W.H., *The History of Magherafelt,* Moyola Books, Co. Londonderry, reprinted 1988.

Men of the Times, South Africa, Cape edition, 1906, Transvaal edition, 1905.

Morris, Richard B., *Encyclopaedia of American History.*

O'Neill, Capt. Francis (Ed.), *O'Neill's Music of Ireland,* Dan Collins, New York, 1963.

Reid, Richard, From Ballyduff to Boorowa. Irish Assisted Immigration to New South Wales 1830–1896, *The Irish Australians,* The Society of Australian Genealogists and Ulster Historical Foundation, 1984.

Sainty, M.R. and Johnson, K.A. (Eds.), *Census of New South Wales: November 1828,* Library of Australian History, Sydney, 1980.

The Voyage of Henry John Ford from London to Queensland, *Generation,* Vol. 16, No. 3, Genealogical Society of Queensland, 1994

Woodham-Smith, Cecil, *The Great Hunger,* Hamish Hamilton, London, reprinted 1988.

Vine-Hall, Nick, Have You Australian Connections?, *Family Tree Magazine Yearbook,* 1986.

Chapter 5

ARCHIVES

Part 1: Ireland

Introduction

For those visiting Ireland in search of ancestry, a knowledge of the main repositories is essential. It is also important for those engaged in postal research (Chapter 2) to address their enquiries to the correct repository. Most archives have produced publications designed to help researchers identify and locate documents relevant to their enquiries. Readers will find that some of the material listed in pre-1922 publications has been lost or destroyed, in which case they should contact sources concerned for further information. The following is an introduction to the main Irish archives and some of the records held there.

The National Archives (NA)

In 1867, the Public Record Office of Ireland (PROI) was established in the Four Courts complex, Dublin. At that time, its main function was the collection and preservation of wills, Church of Ireland records, records of bodies and organisations over 20 years old and medieval documents. In 1922, during the Civil War, much of this material was destroyed. By 1992, surviving records of the PROI, together with material from the State Paper Office had been transferred to premises in Bishops Street, Dublin, now the headquarters of the newly organised National Archives.

Contents of the NA

In addition to transferred material, the NA contains census returns, *Griffith's Valuation*, Tithe Applotment Books, Church of Ireland parish records, wills and will indexes, government departmental records etc. Information about some of these will be found in Chapter 6.

Publications

(a) *The Public Record: Sources for Local Studies.* Summary of records held in the NA together with a brief historical background to this material.

(b) *Reports of the Deputy Keepers of the Public Records in Ireland.* Numbered consecutively from 1 to 60, these reports list records acquired by the NA during the period 1922–1961. The last report will cover the period 1962 to May 1988 inclusive.

(c) *Reports of the Director of the National Archives.* These supercede (b), above, and list material subsequently acquired by the NA each year. Although to be compiled annually, the first report will cover the period June 1988 to December 1991 inclusive.

Readers' tickets

A reader's ticket will be issued on production of identification showing the reader's address and a statement of research aims.

Photocopying facilities are available and microfilm of specific material can be purchased.

The Public Record Office of Northern Ireland (PRONI)

The Public Record Office of Northern Ireland was created in 1923 to ensure the identification and preservation of important information from official sources in the newly formed state of Northern Ireland. Concerned mainly with these six counties, the material today consists of official records, e.g. papers from government departments, courts, local authorities, public bodies, etc., and material of a private or business nature, e.g. family documents, estate papers, business records, etc. Although most of this material concerns the six counties of Northern Ireland, some of it relates to other parts of Ulster Province (Cavan, Donegal and Monaghan). (See also Chapter 1.)

Contents of the PRONI

Records held by PRONI include Tithe Applotment Books, *Griffith's Valuation* and related material, church records, maps, estate papers, etc., further information about which will be found in Chapter 6.

Publications

(a) *Guide to the Public Record Office of Northern Ireland.* Describes the contents of PRONI and outlines the procedure for obtaining documents. It is available free of charge.

(b) *Reports of the Deputy Keeper of the Records 1960–89.* Comprises consecutive volumes listing records acquired by PRONI during the periods 1960–65, 1966–72, 1973–75, 1976–79 and 1980–89. These have now been superceded by annual reports covering the periods 1990–91, 1991–92, etc.

(c) *Guides.* A series of guides to classes or types of records are now being produced. These include *Guide to Educational Records; Guide to Cabinet Conclusions; Guide to Sources for Womens' History,* etc.

PRONI have also published educational facsimile packs illustrating aspects of Irish history that have particular relevance to the Province of Ulster. These are available for purchase.

Readers' tickets

These can be applied for in advance or issued at the time of the first visit. They are issued per calendar year, i.e. from January 1st.

Other facilities

A personal photocopying service is provided. Photocopies of documents may also be obtained by mail provided that correct references are supplied. Customers using this service must first write to PRONI and obtain special order forms.

The National Library of Ireland (NLI)

Established in 1877, the National Library has occupied its present building since 1890. Today it is the main repository for private papers, estate records, printed books, newspapers, maps, periodicals and official publications relating to Ireland. There are also a number of photographic collections.

Publications

In the Historical Documents series:

(a) *The Landed Gentry.* A set of facsimile documents produced in conjunction with an earlier exhibition illustrating business, personal and day-to-day affairs of the landed gentry in Ireland.

(b) *The Land War 1879–1903.* A set of facsimile documents illustrating the involvement of landlords, tenants and the government during the so-called Land War.

There are further titles in this series illustrating aspects of Irish history, much of which contains genealogical information of value to family historians.

More workman's tools

Two sets of indexes provide lists of material available in the NLI and other repositories.

(a) *Manuscript Sources for the History of Irish Civilisation.* Consists of 14 volumes containing brief descriptions of manuscripts of Irish interest in archives and libraries around the world. These include references to estate papers in Irish archives.

(b) *Periodical Sources for the History of Irish Civilisation.* Consists of nine volumes listing articles, etc. that appeared in a variety of Irish periodicals up to 1970.

The above volumes (or parts thereof) exist in repositories and libraries around Ireland. Copies will also be found in archives around the world. Descendants overseas should make local enquiries to ascertain availabilty.

Readers' tickets

A reader's ticket may be issued on production of identification and after a personal interview. A photograph will be taken of the applicant. Permission to conduct further research in another part of the library (the manuscript room) may be given subject to further interview.

Other facilities

Copies of some material in the NLI can be obtained by mail provided it can be identified. Researchers are advised to contact the NLI for further details.

The Registry of Deeds (RD)

Established in 1707 to record land and property transactions and also control the ownership of land by Roman Catholics, the RD opened in 1708. Today it contains over 3 million memorials of deeds (see Chapter 6). Unlike many records that were stored elsewhere, those in the RD escaped destruction. The public is allowed access to the Registry of Deeds on payment of a fee.

Contents of the RD

See Chapter 6.

Readers' tickets

A readers ticket is required.

Other facilities

Photocopies of memorials can be obtained for a fee. The RD also supply photocopies by mail provided that correct references are supplied for a successful search. Postal searches cannot be conducted for material prior to 1833.

The Genealogical Office (GO)

The Genealogical Office in Dublin was established in 1552 as The Office of Arms, its function being to establish and record which Irish families were legally entitled to coats of arms. This was later extended to include duties connected with certain ceremonial events. Renamed the Genealogical Office in 1943, its function today is mainly heraldic. The GO contains material mainly connected with heraldry and the registration of pedigrees. Its records are not available to the general public but many of them can be seen on microfilm in the NA.

Consultancy service

The GO does not conduct family history research but clients seeking guidance about research on individual families may obtain a personal consultation on payment of a fee. This includes the issue of an Ancestry Tracing Research Pack containing relevant information and worksheets. The pack can be obtained separately. Consultation may also be conducted by mail upon receipt of an application form and fee. Further information can be obtained from the GO.

Research service

The secretary of The Association of Professional Genealogists in Ireland (APGI) can be contacted at the Genealogical Office. See Chapter 2 for more information about APGI.

The Valuation Office (VO)

Established in 1852 to supervise the valuation of land by Sir Richard Griffith (see Chapter 6), the Valuation Office has continued to record details of land ownership and valuation up to the present day.

Contents of the VO

The Primary Valuation of Tenements (Griffith's Valuation) together with surveyors' notebooks and related maps are stored here. The public are permitted to examine these records on payment of a fee. Further information about material in the VO will be found in Chapter 6.

Other facilities

Photocopies of documents and maps can be obtained on payment of a fee.

The General Register Office (GRO)

The General Register Office, Dublin is the central repository for the registration of births, marriages and deaths in Ireland as described in Chapter 6. Further information will be found in that chapter. Certificates relating to the above events may be obtained from the GRO.

The Indexes

The public are permitted to examine the GRO's indexes on payment of a fee.

Other facilities

Enquiries and orders for certificates can be conducted by mail provided sufficient information is supplied for a successful search together with the relevant fee.

The General Register Office of Northern Ireland (GRONI)

The General Register Office of Northern Ireland is the central repository for the registration of births, marriages and deaths in Northern Ireland as described in Chapter 6. Further information will be found in that chapter.

The Indexes
The public is allowed to search the GRONI's indexes without charge.

Other facilities
Enquiries and orders for certificates can also be conducted personally or by mail provided sufficient information is supplied for a successful search.

Part 2: Overseas

Sources outside Ireland

Irish descendants resident in or visiting Britain have a unique advantage over those travelling to Ireland for the purpose of research, centuries of immigration having littered England with Irish material (Chapters 3, 6 and 7). Some repositories in London are worthy of particular mention.

The Public Record Office, London (PRO): a source for Irish research

During the British administration of Ireland, official correspondence flowed between government departments in Dublin and London and Irish-related records were created by British departments exercising functions in Ireland. Consequently, departmental records of the British government subsequently transferred to the PRO contain much material relating to Ireland. Certain other records created in Dublin were transferred to the PRO following the creation of the Irish Free State in 1922. Generally, material dating before c.1780 is stored in the repository in Chancery Lane. Later material will be found in Kew. (There are some exceptions to this rule.)

Contents of the PRO
Irish material in the PRO is too vast to record here but includes records of the Royal Irish Constabulary (RIC) (Chapter 6), Irish militias, transportation records, emigratory material, and maps and plans.

The indexes
(a) *Information leaflets.* These provide an introduction and historical background to specific classes of records held at the PRO.
(b)*Public Record Office Current Guide.* This is a three part guide to all the records held by the PRO.
Part 3 is an alphabetical subject index to Parts 1 and 2 and the main classes of records in the PRO. The headings 'Ireland' and 'Irish' indicate the vast amount of material available. Corresponding reference numbers are shown.
Part 2 contains a brief description of each class of record together with a note of its contents.

Part 1 provides a brief history of government departments that created the records. Readers are then referred to the relevant class lists.

(c) *Class lists.* These are detailed lists of each class and are available on open shelves. From these, readers can ascertain the relevancy of individual items which can subsequently be obtained by using the reference numbers provided.

Publication

A useful guide to Irish records in the PRO is Alice Prochaska's *Irish History from 1700: A Guide to Sources in the Public Record Office,* which lists the main classes of Irish records in the PRO from 1700 together with their description. The book is available from the PRO, the British Records Association and book shops.

Readers' tickets

A reader's ticket may be issued on production of identification such as a British driving licence, banker's card or passport.

Other facilities

Photocopying facilities are available.

The British Library (BL)

An Act of Parliament in 1972 brought together a number of existing bodies, including departments of the former British Museum Library, to establish the British Library. Today, the collections of the British Library include many millions of items from around the world.

Collections of the BL

The library's collections, built on the foundation collections of the British Museum (formed in 1753), have been added to ever since by legal deposit, purchase and donation. The BL contains many departments of which four are of particular interest to researchers of Irish history and genealogy.

Reading Room (humanities and social sciences)

The collections here include books and periodicals from Ireland and items relating to all aspects of Irish life, including literary, biographical, topographical and historical material.

Catalogues

The British (Museum) Library's *General Catalogue of Printed Books* lists material acquired up to 1975 and consists of large volumes in circular racks in the Reading Room. The *Current Catalogue* on microfiche includes material published after that date. Both catalogues are available on computer terminals situated within the BL.

Official Publications and Social Science Service

This is the reading room for the BL's official publications, which include British Parliamentary Papers on open shelves. *Griffith's Valuation* is also available on microfiche. (See Chapter 6.)

Catalogues

Most of the official publications are catalogued under the relevant country or inter-governmental organisation. For those publications not fully catalogued, a number of supplementary catalogues have been prepared. Advice can be sought from library staff. Various indexes to parliamentary papers are available on open shelves. For the period 1801–1900, the section on Ireland in Vol. IV of the *Subject Catalogue to House of Commons Sessional Papers,* published by Chadwyck-Healey, is invaluable.

Map Library

The collection includes maps and charts, plans and topographical drawings from all parts of the world and includes Ordnance Survey maps of Ireland.

Catalogues

The British (Museum) Library's *Catalogue of Maps, Charts and Plans* lists material acquired up to 1964. It is arranged by country, state, county, town or other geographical area; a supplement was published covering acquisitions up to 1974. The British Library's *Catalogue of Cartographic Materials* lists acquisitions from 1975 to date and is available on microfiche.

Manuscript collections

These collections contain many manuscripts relating to the history, topography, genealogy and literary history of Ireland.

Catalogues

For the manuscript collections, there is a series of printed catalogues arranged under appropriate headings and a class catalogue. There is also a *Catalogue of Irish Manuscripts in the British Museum* published in three volumes in 1926–1953.

Admission

Admission to the BL is generally by photographic pass only. This is given to those needing to see material not readily available elsewhere or researchers requiring the facilities of a large research library. Applicants must produce evidence of identity and two passport-size colour photographs. A supplementary pass is required for access to the manuscript collections. Visitors to the Map Library may apply direct to that office for temporary admission.

Please note. Due to the recent opening of new premises at St. Pancras and transfer of material from the old building, intending readers are advised to write or telephone prior to visiting either library. Only the basic catalogues have been noted above. There are many more available, some of them unpublished. Curatorial staff on duty will be pleased to advise.

The British Library Newspaper Library (BLNL)

The BLNL is part of the British Library and is the principal legal deposit library for newspapers in the United Kingdom. From 1869, copyright law required a copy of every newspaper published in the British Empire to be deposited at the British Museum. In 1905, most of the collection was transferred to the present site at Colindale in north-west London.

Contents of the BLNL

The collection includes English, Welsh, Scottish and Irish national and local newspapers from 1700 onwards, though in the early years holdings are by no means complete, and a large collection of Commonwealth and foreign newspapers. British weekly and fortnightly magazines and popular periodicals are also held.

Catalogue
The collection is listed in the *Catalogue of the Newspaper Library,* which is arranged both by country and town of publication and by title. Ireland (both the Republic and Northern Ireland) is very well represented. Newspapers published in the Irish Republic are still received under the legal deposit legislation.

Admission
Members of the public aged over 18 are admitted on production of proof of indentity. A reader's ticket may then be issued.

The Irish Genealogical Research Society (IGRS)

Established in 1936 to promote and encourage the study of Irish genealogy and attempt to overcome some of the losses of 1922, the IGRS has become one of the foremost organisations concerned with Irish research. Situated at its library in London, the IGRS has members around the world.

Contents of the IGRS
The IGRS library contains collections of books and other material relating to Irish genealogy. The many items include *Griffith's Valuation,* Will indexes and abstracts, the 1901 *Townland Index* , biographies on Irish surnames and journals of research societies in Ireland. There are also collections of Irish manuscripts dating from the 19th century and printed material from the 17th century onward. Indexes are available for some of this material. Members and others are encouraged to deposit details of their research for the benefit of other library users.

Other facilities
Photocopying facilities are available.

Publication
The Irish Genealogist, published annually since 1937, contains news of the society, articles of genealogical interest and reviews of books and other publications. It is distributed to members around the world. A newsletter is also produced several times each year.

Membership
An annual membership fee permits members to visit the society's library during opening times. A visitor's fee is charged for non-members. At present, the IGRS library is only open on Saturday afternoons.

Branches
The Ireland branch of the IGRS holds regular meetings at which visiting speakers give talks on a variety of subjects. Visits are also organised to archives and other locations. The branch produces its own newsletter.

Further Information
It should be emphasised that researchers will need a basic knowledge of Irish research and have conducted preliminary enquiries in order to gain the most from visiting the IGRS library.

The Society of Genealogists (SOG)

Founded in England in 1911 to promote and encourage the study of genealogy and heraldry, the Society of Genealogists is now one of the foremost organisations concerned with genealogical research. The society's library contains material dating from the 16th century up to and beyond the commencement of English civil registration in 1837.

Contents of the SOG

The Society's collections include a large quantity of Irish material which is listed in a booklet published by the SOG (see *Publication,* below). Also of interest to Irish descendants are the microfilmed copies of civil registration indexes for (a) Scotland: 1855–1920, and (b) England/Wales: 1837–1920, in which many emigrants from Ireland will be found.

Publication

Sources for Irish Genealogy in the Society of Genealogists, a booklet compiled by the Director, Anthony Camp, listing Irish material in the SOG library. Material is indexed by county. At the time of writing, the booklet was out of print but currently under revision.

Admission

Admission to the Society is by annual membership or a visitor's fee.

Sources overseas

There are many sources around the world holding Irish or Irish-related material and readers are encouraged to visit archives in their respective countries to identify them. To encourage research, the author lists three sources overseas together with a brief indication of some of the material held.

The United States of America: The Library of Congress

The primary function of the Library of Congress is to serve Members of Congress and thereafter, the needs of the government, libraries, members of the public, Universities and learned societies. The services provided by the Library of Congress do not include conducting research in heraldry or family history. Amongst the collections are published material relating to Ireland and aspects of Irish life. There are a number of departments containing items of interest to Irish researchers. These include:

The Local History and Genealogy (LH&G) Room

Griffith's Valuation on microfiche (Chapter 6).

Microform Reading Room

British Parliamentary Papers on microfilm (Chapter 6).

Geography and Map Reading Room

Ordnance survey maps of Ireland.

An unindexed collection of Irish genealogical material microfilmed at the National Library in Dublin.

Catalogues

Researchers interested in Irish genealogy or local history should first visit the Computer Catalogue Center situated, at the time of writing, in the John Adams Building and consult the

Main Card Catalogue. Examples of appropriate subject headings indicating availability of material in the library are: Genealogy; Heraldry, Ireland; Register of Births, etc., Dublin.

Admission

The reading room is open to the public subject to conditions. Readers should contact the library for further information about accessibility and material.

Canada: The National Archives of Canada

Founded in 1872, the function of the National Archives is to acquire, preserve and make available to researchers material of historical interest. Among this material are copies of documents relating to Canadian history, the originals of which are in the possession of other governments including Great Britain and Ireland. The collections include (a) ordnance survey maps of Ireland, (b) *British Parliamentary Papers,* (c) some immigration records 1817–1831, (d) ship passenger lists 1865–1919. (See also Chapter 4.)

Publication

Tracing Your Ancestors in Canada. A general guide to genealogical research in Canada with particular reference to material in the National Archives.

Admission

A research pass is required for access to the reading rooms.

Australia: The Genealogical Society of Victoria (GSV)

As stated elsewhere in this volume (Chapters 4 and 7), the GSV holds a vast quantity of material relating to Australian settlement. This includes records connected with transportation, employment and a variety of other material listing Irishmen and women. Specific Irish material includes (a) *Griffith's Valuation* on microfiche, and (b) *Tithe Applotment Books* on microfiche

Publication

Ancestor contains articles and other information relating mainly to Australian settlement with particular reference to the State of Victoria. Items relating to English and Irish research are frequently included. The GSV have formed an 'Irish Ancestry Group' (IAG) assisting members who have Irish interests. The IAG produce their own publication, *Blarney,* a newsletter containing items of interest for those of Irish descent.

Activities

Activities of the GSV and IAG are advertised in their respective publications.

Admission to the GSV

By membership.

Please note. Only a brief reference has been made to 'finding aids' and publications of the repositories described. Visitors may discover others relevant to their research. The location of repositories are shown in Appendix B. Further information about Irish records will be found in Chapter 6.

Bibliography

Ancestor, Journal of the Genealogical Society of Victoria (GSV).

Blarney, Vol. 3, No. 3, Irish Ancestry Group Inc., 1991 (an inaugural member society of the GSV).

Camp, Anthony, *Sources for Irish Genealogy in the Society of Genealogists,* Society of Genealogists, London, 1990.

Guide to the Public Record Office of Northern Ireland, PRONI, Belfast, 1991.

The Irish Genealogist, Irish Genealogical Research Society, London. (Published annually.)

Janine, Roy, *Tracing Your Ancestors in Canada,* Minister of Supply and Services, Canada, 9th edn., 1988.

The Landed Gentry, National Library of Ireland, Dublin, 1979.

The Land War 1879–1903, National Library of Ireland, Dublin, 1976.

The National Library of Ireland (leaflet), NLI, Dublin.

McCarthy, Tony (Ed.), *Irish Roots,* Vols. 1 and 2, Belgrave Publications, Cork.

Prochaska, Alice, *Irish History from 1700: A Guide to Sources in the Public Record Office,* British Records Association, London, 1986.

Public Record Office, Current Guide: Parts 1–3, HMSO, London.

Short Guide to the National Archives, The National Archives, Dublin.

Chapter 6

IRISH RECORDS

A myth destroyed

Contrary to popular belief, Irish research is not impossible. Many records survived the destructions and these are available today in Irish archives. Opinions vary as to their worth, many people having difficulty tracing their origins to before the 19th century. Others discover ancestry going back centuries, so the possibilities are there.

A visit to Ireland

With luck, your research in the host country (see Chapter 3) will have been successful and you now possess information about your ancestor(s) and their origin. You may also have an opportunity to visit Ireland for research purposes, or as part of a tour or holiday during which you can 'indulge' to your heart's content.

The Irish language

The Irish language is unlikely to cause you problems, and the fact that most surviving pre-1922 records are written in English will encourage those who were apprehensive about translation. From 1922, when 26 Irish counties obtained a measure of independence, the Irish language was used more frequently in official records; a factor that may influence future research.

What records are available?

This chapter describes some of the available records, offers advice on their use, and locates some of the sources where they can be found.

The Irish census returns

Census returns: 1821–1891
The first organised census of Ireland commenced in 1821. Further censuses were held every 10 years until 1911 and thereafter at irregular intervals. Unfortunately, most of the 1821–1891 returns were pulped into waste paper during the First World War (Ireland being part of the United Kingdom at that time) or destroyed during the Civil War in 1922. These returns would have benefitted today's family historians and their loss has contributed to many of the problems, real and imaginary, of Irish research.

Sources
The returns for a small number of parishes have survived, and details of these can be obtained from (a) The National Archives, Dublin (NA), (b) The Public Record Office of Northern Ireland, Belfast (PRONI), and (c) The National Library of Ireland, Dublin (NLI).

Census returns: 1901 and 1911
Probably the best known of surviving records are the census returns for 1901 and 1911. Their usefulness was enhanced by the earlier destructions for they show the names and ages of many people born during the 19th century. The returns for each dwelling lists all persons, including visitors, who were present on census night, showing their county of birth (if born

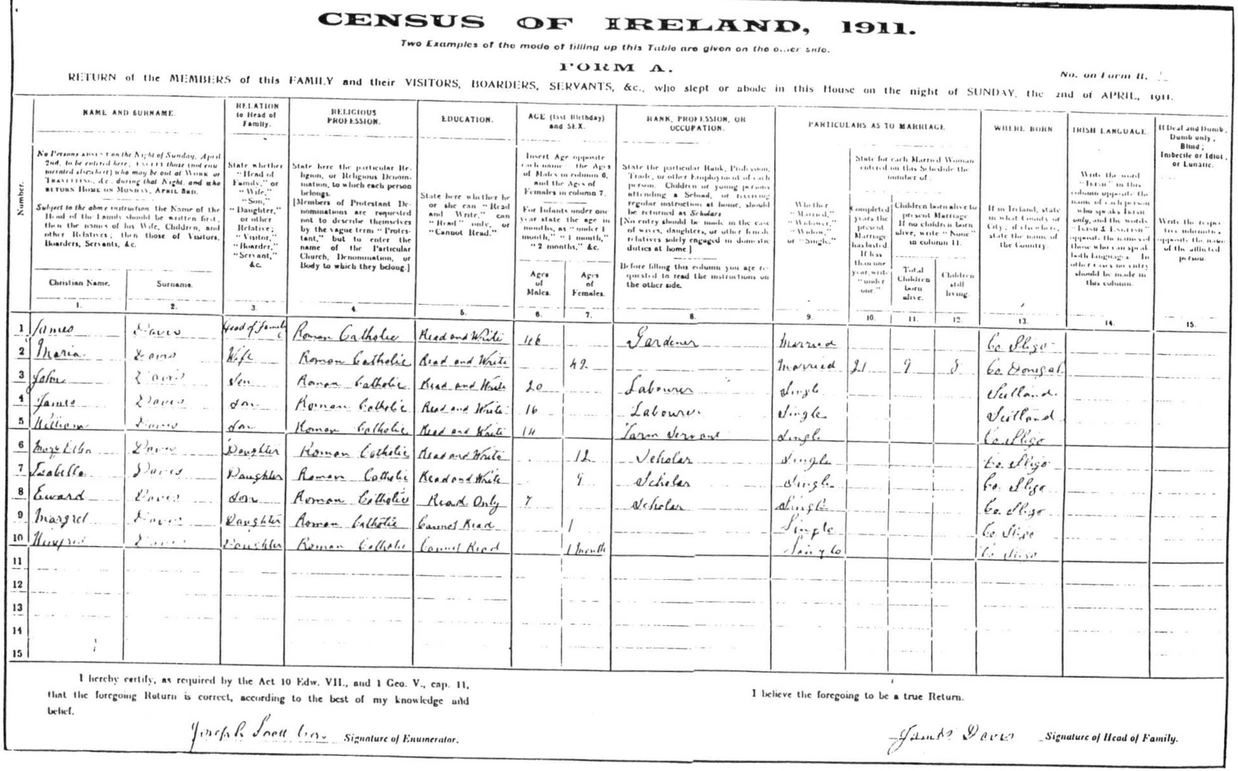

CENSUS OF IRELAND, 1911.

Two Examples of the mode of filling up this Table are given on the other side.

FORM A.

No. on Form B. [illegible]

RETURN of the MEMBERS of this FAMILY and their VISITORS, BOARDERS, SERVANTS, &c., who slept or abode in this House on the night of SUNDAY, the 2nd of APRIL, 1911.

Number	Christian Name (1)	Surname (2)	Relation to Head of Family (3)	Religious Profession (4)	Education (5)	Ages of Males (6)	Ages of Females (7)	Rank, Profession, or Occupation (8)	Whether "Married," "Widower," "Widow," or "Single." (9)	Completed years the present Marriage has lasted (10)	Total Children born alive (11)	Children still living (12)	Where Born (13)	Irish Language (14)	If Deaf and Dumb; Dumb only; Blind; Imbecile or Idiot; or Lunatic (15)
1	James	[illegible]	Head of Family	Roman Catholic	Read and Write	46		Gardener	Married				Co. Sligo		
2	Maria	[illegible]	Wife	Roman Catholic	Read and Write		42		Married	21	9	8	Co. Donegal		
3	John	[illegible]	Son	Roman Catholic	Read and Write	20		Labourer	Single				Scotland		
4	James	[illegible]	Son	Roman Catholic	Read and Write	16		Labourer	Single				Scotland		
5	William	[illegible]	Son	Roman Catholic	Read and Write	14		Farm Servant	Single				Co. Sligo		
6	Mary Ellen	[illegible]	Daughter	Roman Catholic	Read and Write		12	Scholar	Single				Co. Sligo		
7	Isabella	[illegible]	Daughter	Roman Catholic	Read and Write		9	Scholar	Single				Co. Sligo		
8	Edward	[illegible]	Son	Roman Catholic	Read Only	7		Scholar	Single				Co. Sligo		
9	Margret	[illegible]	Daughter	Roman Catholic	Cannot Read		1		Single				Co. Sligo		
10	[illegible]	[illegible]	Daughter	Roman Catholic	Cannot Read		1 month		Single				Co. Sligo		
11															
12															
13															
14															
15															

I hereby certify, as required by the Act 10 Edw. VII., and 1 Geo. V., cap. 11, that the foregoing Return is correct, according to the best of my knowledge and belief.

Joseph [illegible] — Signature of Enumerator.

I believe the foregoing to be a true Return.

James [illegible] — Signature of Head of Family.

Fig. 6.1. 1911 census return for Branchfield, nr. Ballymote, Co. Sligo, Eire.

in Ireland) and country of birth (if born outside Ireland). Family historians will be surprised at the number of people born elsewhere in the United Kingdom. The returns are arranged by Poor Law Union, electoral division, county, barony, parish and townland (or street if in a town or city). When consulting these in the NA, you need only quote the county and townland, indexes on the open shelves enable returns to be located with ease. Where more than one townland of the same name exists in a county, the parish is also required. House numbers were allocated to dwellings in country areas, but as these were based on the direction taken by enumerators, they vary in each census. In cities and towns, house numbers are shown in the usual way.

Sources
Copies of the the returns for the six counties of Northern Ireland are not yet available in the PRONI but returns for the whole of Ireland will be found in the NA. Some county libraries hold copies relevant to their areas.

Civil registration

Civil Registration is another factor contributing to the difficulties of Irish research; the registration of certain marriages in 1845 and the later introduction of full registration resulting in confusion for today's family historians. The following is a synopsis of civil registration in Ireland.

1845. Civil registration of non-Catholic marriages began and included not only (protestant) Anglicans, but also the marriages of Presbyterians, Wesleyans, Jews, etc., in fact all those who were not Roman Catholic.

1864. Civil registration was extended to include Roman Catholic marriages, and the religious distinction was dropped. From this date, full registration began and all births, marriages and deaths were required to be registered.

Historical events complicated matters even further. From 1922, when Southern Ireland obtained 'independence', Northern Ireland remained part of the United Kingdom, retaining its own birth, marriage and death records. Enquiries concerning these should be directed to the General Register Office of Northern Ireland (GRONI), Belfast.

For the present, however, Irish research is generally concerned with the period before 1922, and these records will be found in the General Register Office (GRO), Dublin. Pre-1922 records for Northern Ireland, with the exceptions shown below, will be found in the General Register Office of Northern Ireland (GRONI). The following will clarify the position:

Marriages

Dates	Record coverage	Archive
1845–1863	Non-Roman Catholic marriages in all Ireland	GRO
1864–1921	All marriages including those of Roman Catholics in all Ireland	GRO
1922–present day	All marriages in the Republic of Ireland only	GRO
1922–present day	All Marriages in Northern Ireland only	GRONI

N.B. Northern Ireland: Original registers of marriages 1845–1921 are still retained by local registrars. Marriage registers from 1922 are retained by GRONI.

Births and deaths

Dates	Record coverage	Archive
1864–1921	Births and deaths in all Ireland	GRO
1922–present day	Births and deaths in the Republic of Ireland only	GRO
1864–present day	Births and deaths in Northern Ireland only	GRONI

Miscellaneous registers

But what about ancestors overseas? In addition to the above, the following registers are also kept by the GRO.

(a) Children born at sea with at least one Irish parent, registered between January 1864 and December 1921.

(b) Children born at sea of Southern Irish parentage from 1921.

(c) Deaths at sea of Irish-born persons, registered between January 1864 and December 1921.

(d) Deaths at sea after 1921 of persons born in Southern Ireland.

(e) Births of children of Irish parentage as certified by British Consuls abroad between January 1864 and December 1921.

(f) Deaths of Irish-born persons as certified by British Consuls abroad between January 1864 and December 1921.

(g) Marriages celebrated by the Rev. J.G.F. Schulze of the German Protestant Church, Poolbeg St., Dublin between 1806 and 1837.

(h) Adoptions registered in the Irish Republic from 10th July 1953

(i) Certain marriages at Lourdes.

(j) Births, marriages and deaths of Irish subjects serving in the British Army abroad.

(k) Certain other births, marriages and deaths under various legislation.

Similar registers are kept by GRONI.

(a) Children born at sea with at least one parent born in Northern Ireland, registered from 1st January 1922.

(b) Deaths at sea from 1st January 1922 of persons born in Northern Ireland.

(c) Births of children with Northern Ireland parents as registered with British Consuls abroad from 1st January 1922.

(d) Deaths of persons born in Northern Ireland as registered by British consuls abroad from 1st January 1922.

(e) Marriages abroad of persons born in Northern Ireland as registered by British consuls from 1st January 1923.

(f) Births, marriages and deaths of persons born in Northern Ireland as registered by British High Commissioners in Commonwealth countries from 1st January 1950.

Name and Registration District	Vol.	Page
KELLY, Honora. Thurles	8	765
—— Honora. Kilrush	4	318
—— Honora. Claremorris	19	174
—— Honora. Enniscorthy	14	718
—— Honora. Cork	15	191
—— Honora. Longford	18	234
—— Honora. Youghal	19	938
—— Honora. Claremorris	19	173
—— Honora. Cork	10	179
—— Honora. Listowel	10	556
—— Honoria. Kilrush	19	368
—— Honoria. Loughrea	19	397
—— Honoria. Castlereagh	9	156
—— Honoria. Strokestown	8	425
—— Honoria. Mountbellew	9	430
—— Hubert. Mountbellew	19	236
—— Hugh. Dromore West	13	362
—— Hugh. Roscommon	17	55
—— Hugh. Dunfanaghy	17	235
—— Hugh. Manorhamilton	17	240
—— Hugh. Manorhamilton	3	107
—— Hugh. Clogher	16	258
—— Hugh. Belfast	11	674
—— Hugh. Magherafelt	8	723
—— Hugh. Granard	2	231
—— Hugh. Omagh	6	759
—— Isabella. Lurgan	11	207
—— Isabella. Banbridge	6	143
—— Isabella. Ballymena	12	892
—— Isabella Margaret. Naas	4	107
—— James. Castlebar	4	80
—— James. Boyle	4	45
—— James. Ballinrobe	4	829
—— James. Waterford	4	356
—— James. Mountbellew	19	410
—— James. Mountbellew	13	577
—— James. Edenderry	13	415
—— James. Athy	13	623
—— James. Nenagh	13	746
—— James. Tullamore	13	548
—— James. Kilkenny	13	543
—— James. Kilkenny	9	654
—— James. Cloghen	9	255
—— James. Ennis	19	38
—— James. Ballinasloe	14	531
—— James. Tobercurry	14	551
—— James. Tuam	14	503
—— James. Callan	14	152
—— James. Castlereagh	14	494
—— James. Swineford	2	589
—— James. Dublin, South	17	80
—— James. Enniskillen	17	342
—— James. Strabane	7	812
—— James. Dublin, South	7	935
—— James. Naas	18	119
—— James. Cavan	18	13
—— James. Athlone	18	726
—— James. Urlingford	18	443
—— James. Carlow	6	821
—— James. Newry	19	646
—— James. Dungarvan	19	567
—— James. Tuam	5	467
—— James. Limerick	12	843
—— James. Gorey	12	510
—— James. Drogheda	5	5
—— James. Bandon	3	12
—— James. Athlone	12	233
—— James. Manorhamilton	10	385
—— James. Killarney	17	463
—— James. Carrickmacross	17	797
—— James. Dundalk	17	409
—— James. Baulieborough	17	784
—— James. Dublin, South	7	1060
—— James. Rathdown	7	1014
—— James. Rathdown	7	573
—— James. Dublin, North	1	445
—— James. Dungannon	1	310
—— James. Belfast	12	234
—— James. Manorhamilton	12	24
—— James. Castlederg	2	390
—— James. Baltinglass	2	100
—— James. Gortin	12	330
—— James. Sligo	3	213
—— James. Longford	3	14
—— James. Athlone	16	618
—— James. Lisburn	16	207
—— James. Banbridge	16	306
—— James. Belfast	11	795
—— James. Newtownards	11	294
—— James. Belfast	11	23
—— James. Antrim	11	687
—— James. Magherafelt	11	488
—— James. Dungannon	17	943
—— James. Rathdown	2	584
—— James. Dublin, South	2	862
—— James. Shillelagh	2	34
—— James. Donegal	19	909
—— James Dennis. Wexford	1	1014
—— James Johnston. Downpatrick	17	1029
—— James Joseph. Dublin, North	6	647

Name and Registration District	Vol.	Page
KELLY, Johanna. Limerick	20	415
—— Johanna. Donaghmore	13	519
—— Johanna. Mitchelstown	4	724
—— Johanna. Tralee	2	715
—— Johanna. Listowel	10	335
—— Johanna. Thurles	18	640
—— Johanna. Kilkenny	3	521
—— Johannah. Macroom	10	560
—— John. Castlebar	4	106
—— John. Castlebar	4	112
—— John. Wexford	4	850
—— John. Dungarvan	4	591
—— John. Glennamaddy	19	332
—— John. Westport	19	593
—— John. Mullingar	13	325
—— John. Galway	19	289
—— John. Kilrush	19	386
—— John. Strokestown	13	583
—— John. Monaghan	13	291
—— John. Strokestown	13	395
—— John. Athlone	13	22
—— John. Athlone	13	15
—— John. Parsonstown	13	645
—— John. Carrick-on-Suir	19	628
—— John. Castlereagh	9	162
—— John. Castlereagh	9	147
—— John. Mountbellew	14	655
—— John. Ballinrobe	14	50
—— John. Clifden	9	506
—— John. Castlebar	9	131
—— John. Mitchelstown	9	853
—— John. Tuam	9	532
—— John. Ballina	9	10
—— John. Enniscorthy	9	738
—— John. Waterford	9	959
—— John. Castlereagh	9	154
—— John. Carrick-on-Suir	14	625
—— John. Ballinrobe	14	50
—— John. Castlereagh	14	149
—— John. Castlereagh	14	145
—— John. Carrick-on-Suir	14	610
—— John. Thomastown	14	844
—— John. Waterford	14	861
—— John. Mountbellew	14	402
—— John. Claremorris	14	176
—— John. Swineford	14	487
—— John. Loughrea	14	390
—— John. Ballinasloe	14	26
—— John. Clifden	14	191
—— John. Kenmare	15	276
—— John. Kilmallock	15	279
—— John. Castlebar	4	113
—— John. New Ross	4	771
—— John. Killadysert	9	341
—— John. Youghal	19	1026
—— John. Ballinasloe	9	58
—— John. Carrick-on-Suir	9	629
—— John. Castlereagh	9	162
—— John. Omagh	2	235
—— John. Londonderry	17	176
—— John. Rathdown	17	956
—— John. Millford	17	253
—— John. Londonderry	17	223
—— John. Tullamore	8	818
—— John. Kilrush	4	431
—— John. Swineford	4	430
—— John. Swineford	4	436
—— John. Athlone	18	15
—— John. Granard	18	205
—— John. Drogheda	7	538
—— John. Granard	7	163
—— John. Glenties	7	116
—— John. Enniskillen	7	87
—— John. Armagh	5	63
—— John. Castlecomer	18	492
—— John. Mohill	18	257
—— John. Tipperary	18	687
—— John. Tullamore	18	717
—— John. Magherafelt	6	809
—— John. Manorhamilton	17	238
—— John. Sligo	7	336
—— John. Thomastown	19	867
—— John. New Ross	19	842
—— John. Clonmel	19	612
—— John. Galway	19	292
—— John. Killarney	3	317
—— John. Cork	15	135
—— John. Parsonstown	3	422
—— John. Londonderry	12	204
—— John. Manorhamilton	12	237
—— John. Dublin, North	12	211
—— John. Sligo	12	318
—— John. Granard	3	184
—— John. Naas	12	877
—— John. Dublin, North	12	557
—— John. Kilmallock	16	428
—— John. Kilmallock	16	407

Name and Registration District	Vol.	Page
KELLY, John. Newtownlimavady		
—— John. Larne		
—— John. Strabane		
—— John. Dublin, North		
—— John. Glenties		
—— John. Omagh		
—— John. Belfast		
—— John. Cork		
—— John. Edenderry		
—— John. Parsonstown		
—— John. Monaghan		
—— John. Roscommon		
—— John. Roscommon		
—— John. Castleblayney		
—— John. Newry		
—— John. Newry		
—— John. Dungannon		
—— John. Ballymena		
—— John. Kilkeel		
—— John. Granard		
—— John. Strokestown		
—— John. Athy		
—— John. Castlecomer		
—— John. Carlow		
—— John. Athy		
—— John. Naas		
—— John. Dublin, South		
—— John. Omagh		
—— John. Manorhamilton		
—— John Joseph. Monaghan		
—— John Paul. Downpatrick		
—— John William. Dublin, South		
—— Joseph. Loughrea		
—— Joseph. Mountsellick		
—— Joseph. Carrick-on-Shannon		
—— Joseph. Roscommon		
—— Joseph. Dungarvan		
—— Joseph. Drogheda		
—— Joseph. Dublin, North		
—— Joseph. Carrickmacross		
—— Joseph. Balrothery		
—— Joseph. Dublin, South		
—— Joseph. Balrothery		
—— Joseph. Navan		
—— Joseph. Kells		
—— Joseph. Limerick		
—— Joseph. Rathdrum		
—— Joseph. Edenderry		
—— Joseph. Dublin, South		
—— Joseph. Dungannon		
—— Joseph. Coleraine		
—— Joseph. Armagh		
—— Joseph. Armagh		
—— Joseph. Castleblayney		
—— Joseph. Magherafelt		
—— Joseph. Edenderry		
—— Joseph. Mullingar		
—— Joseph. Longford		
—— Joseph. Dundalk		
—— Joseph James. Dublin, North		
—— Joseph Patrick. Dublin, North		
—— Josephine. Dublin, North		
—— Josephine Mary. Drogheda		
—— Judith. Killala		
—— Julia. Dublin, South		
—— Julia. Navan		
—— Julia. Rathdown		
—— Julia. Killarney		
—— Julia. Cahersiveen		
—— Julia. Bandon		
—— Julia. Newry		
—— Julia. Dublin, South		
—— Kate. Urlingford		
—— Kate. Clonford		
—— Kate. Kilmacthomas		
—— Kate. Ballinasloe		
—— Kate. Roscommon		
—— Kate. Roscommon		
—— Kate. Nenagh		
—— Keata. Cahersiveen		
—— Kerin. Ballinasloe		
—— Latitia. Inishowen		
—— Laurence. Cork		
—— Laurence. Waterford		
—— Laurence. Rathdown		
—— Laurence. Dublin, South		
—— Lawrence. Shillelagh		
—— Lena. Ballymena		
—— Lucinda. Clogher		
—— Lucy. Tullamore		
—— Manus. Galway		
—— Marcella. Dublin, South		
—— Margaret. Ballinahon		
—— Margaret. Athlone		
—— Margaret. Loughrea		
—— Margaret. Loughrea		
—— Margaret. Portumna		
—— Margaret. Glennamaddy		

Fig. 6.2. Extract from the 1864 Index to Irish Births.

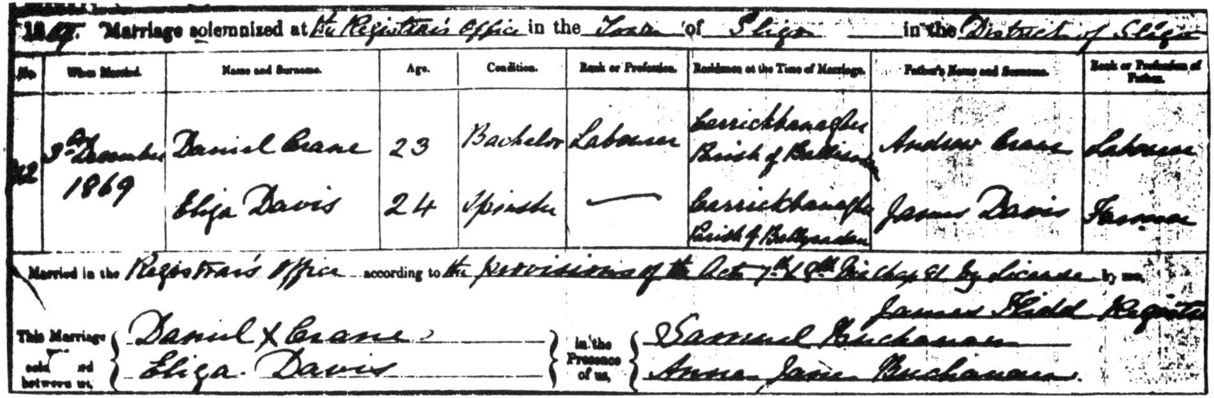

Fig. 6.3. Photocopies from GRO marriage and birth registers.

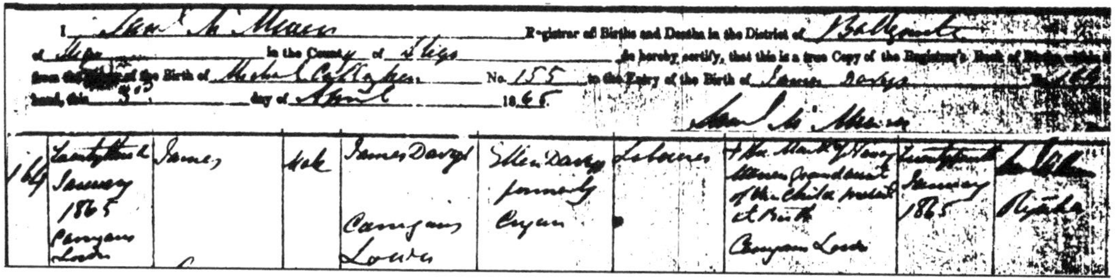

49

(g) Deaths of persons on War Service between 1939 and 1948 who were born in Northern Ireland.

(h) Deaths on board HM ships during the period 1922–54 of persons born in Northern Ireland.

(i) Legal adoptions registered from 1st January 1931.

(j) Still-births registered from 1st January 1961. (Only mother can request details.)

(k) Births, marriages and deaths of Northern Ireland subjects serving in the British Army abroad from 1st January 1927.

The indexes

A fee is charged by the GRO for the examination of its indexes. These are arranged in yearly and quarterly volumes listing surnames, first names or initials and registration districts, together with the volume and page numbers of the entries. Similar indexes are kept by GRONI to which the public has ready access.

Certificates and photocopies

The GRO and GRONI provide certificates in the usual manner if sufficient information is supplied to identify an entry. The GRO will supply, upon request, photocopies of register entries. Enquirers should contact them to ascertain fees.

An alternative source

Relatively unknown sources for Irish research are the family history centres of the Church of Jesus Christ of Latter Day Saints. Some of these possess microfilmed copies of the Irish indexes to births, marriages and deaths which are available for consultation without charge. These enable family historians to obtain details of entries without travelling to Ireland, and obtain certificates from the GRO/GRONI by mail. (See also Chapter 2.) For further information about family history centres, see the section **Census substitutes** later in this chapter.

Estate records

Estate papers

The administration of estates on which most of the Irish population lived generated thousands of documents including bills, rentals, accounts, letters, etc. Such material contains a variety of information; rentals for example, listing the names of tenants and rents that were due. Other documents concerned with administration may also refer to individual tenants or local tradesmen with whom business was conducted. Many of these documents have survived and can be seen today in the NA and NLI. Others are retained in private collections.

Another workman's tool

An invaluable tool for identifying and locating estate records is *Manuscript Sources for the History of Irish Civilisation*. The 11 volumes and a three volume supplement have been described as 'the only comprehensive guide' to such records, showing amongst other material, surviving estate papers indexed under the landlord's name and county in which the estate was situated. They also indicate in which repository, the NA or NLI, they will be found. Unfortunately, the volumes only list material coming to notice before 1976.

Encumbered estates

The effects of the Great Famine left many landlords in debt and in many cases, the only solution was to sell their land. This procedure was simplified when conducted through the Encumbered Estates Court (later the Landed Estates Court). To prepare for each sale, maps of the estate were prepared, together with lists of tenants and their rents. In many cases, these included illustrations of the 'big houses' and their surroundings. More than 3,000 estates were sold between 1849 and 1857.

Sources

The NA have a small collection of estate papers but a larger collection will be found in the NLI. The PRONI have a collection relating to Northern Ireland. Papers relating to encumbered estates and known as the Landed Estate Court Records, will be found in the NA. Unfortunately, Landed Estate Court Records dating between 1849 and 1857 are not listed in *Manuscript Sources for the History of Irish Civilisation*. This publication will be found in the NA, NLI and PRONI. The complete collection, or parts thereof, may also be found in archives around the world.

Griffith's Valuation of Ireland

The Primary Valuation of Ireland, popularly known as *Griffith's Valuation,* was a survey of land and property carried out in each county under the supervision of a noted geologist and civil engineer, Sir Richard Griffith. The survey was carried out between 1846 and 1865, its purpose being to establish a means by which a tax could be calculated for the upkeep of the poor. The results were published and copies are available today in the National Archives, Dublin (NA) and other sources around Ireland.

Arranged in county order, the survey lists names of landowners and tenants, plus the extent and valuation of their property. The returns are further arranged by Poor Law Union, (groups of parishes with a 'central' workhouse) barony, parish and townland. In order to search these returns efficiently, it is necessary to have a basic understanding of this arrangement. (See Chapter 1.)

The General Index of Surnames

There was no index to *Griffith's Valuation* until the National Library compiled their typewritten *General Index of Surnames* also known as the *Householders' Index.* Arranged in separate volumes for each county, these show recorded surnames and their frequency, i.e. the number of times each appears in a particular area. The *General Index* will help researchers to discover, by a process of elimination

(a) the baronies in which a given surname appears,

(b) the parishes in which that surname will be found, and

(c) valuation documents in which parishes, townlands, and individuals are clearly shown.

The meaning of G and T

The letter G shown in the index, refers to a surname appearing in *Griffith's Valuation*. The number following refers to the number of times that surname was recorded in a particular barony or parish. A single occurrence is shown as G (not G1). G2 means that a surname appears on two occasions etc. The letter T means a surname appears in the Tithe Applotment books which are described elsewhere in this chapter. The more frequently a given surname appears, the more difficult will be the task of tracing an individual because first names are

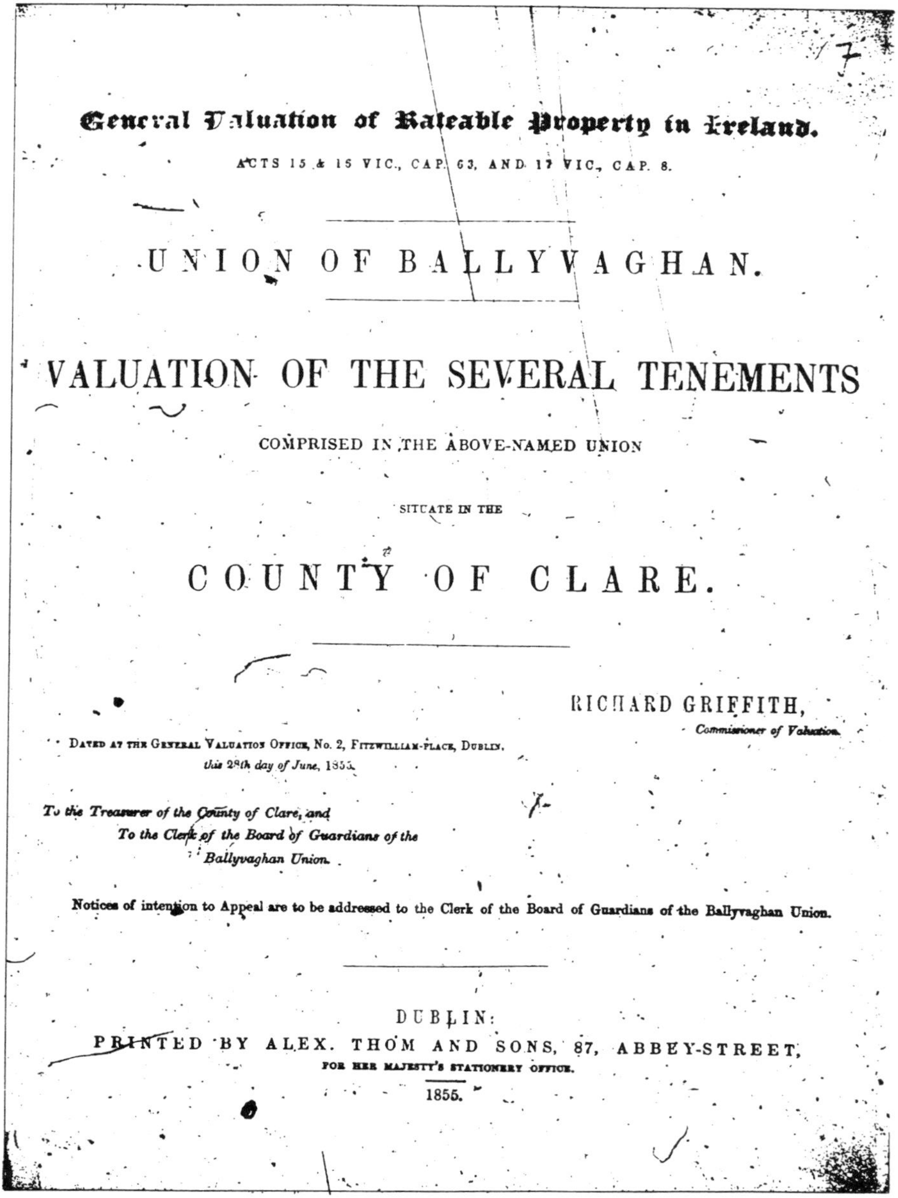

General Valuation of Rateable Property in Ireland.

ACTS 15 & 15 VIC., CAP. 63, AND 17 VIC., CAP. 8.

UNION OF BALLYVAGHAN.

VALUATION OF THE SEVERAL TENEMENTS

COMPRISED IN THE ABOVE-NAMED UNION

SITUATE IN THE

COUNTY OF CLARE.

RICHARD GRIFFITH,
Commissioner of Valuation.

DATED AT THE GENERAL VALUATION OFFICE, No. 2, FITZWILLIAM-PLACE, DUBLIN,
this 28th day of June, 1855.

To the Treasurer of the County of Clare, and
To the Clerk of the Board of Guardians of the
Ballyvaghan Union.

Notices of intention to Appeal are to be addressed to the Clerk of the Board of Guardians of the Ballyvaghan Union.

DUBLIN:

PRINTED BY ALEX. THOM AND SONS, 87, ABBEY-STREET,
FOR HER MAJESTY'S STATIONERY OFFICE.

1855.

Fig. 6.4. Title page of *Griffith's Valuation.*

Surname	Code	T	Barony
Adams		T	Bunratty U.
Adams		T	Ibrickan
Adams		T	Islands
Adams	G		Clonderalaw
Adams		T	Moyarta
Adlam	G2	T	Bunratty L.
Aglim	G4	T	Ibrickan
Ahearn	G2	T	Islands
Ahearn	G		Moyarta
Aherin		T	Corcomroe
Ahern		T	Burren
Ahern	G3	T	Corcomroe
Ahern	G	T	Inchiquin
Ahern	G		Bunratty U.
Ahern	G	T	Tulla U.
Ahern	G4		Ibrickan
Ahern	G	T	Islands
Ahern	G6	T	Tulla L.
Ahern	G5	T	Clonderalaw
Aherne	G		Moyarta
Ahern	G5		Bunratty L.
Alender	G	T	Moyarta
Alexander	G		Moyarta
Allen	G2	T	Inchiquin
Allen		T	Bunratty U.
Allen	G3	T	Tulla U.
Allan	G		Islands
Allen	G	T	Tulla L.
Allen	G3		Moyarta
Allon	G		Bunratty L.
Allendan	G		Moyarta
Allender	G4	T	Moyarta
Allison	G		Tulla L.
Allnan	G		Tulla L.
Alpin	G		Burren
Anberson	G		Moyarta
Anderson	G		Corcomroe
Anderson	G		Ibrickan
Anderson	G		Tulla L.
Anderson		T	Bunratty L.
Anglam	G	T	Clonderalaw
Anglec		T	Corcomroe
Anglim		T	Tulla U.
Anglim	G	T	Ibrickan
Anglim	G	T	Tulla L.
Anglim		T	Moyarta
Anglum	G4	T	Clonderalaw
Angly	G	T	Tulla L.
Arby	G	T	Ibrickan
Archdeacon	G		Burren
Archer		T	Islands
Argill	G		Islands
Arkins	G4	T	Corcomroe
Arkins		T	Tulla L.
Armitage	G		Islands
Armitage	G		Moyarta
Armstrong		T	Burren
Armstrong	G		Corcomroe
Armstrong	G2	T	Bunratty U.
Armstrong	G		Tulla U.
Armstrong	G		Ibrickan
Armstrong	G	T	Islands
Armstrong	G		Tulla L.
Armstrong	G5		Moyarta
Armstrong	G	T	Bunratty L.
Arthur		T	Corcomroe
Arthur	G3	T	Inchiquin
Arthur	G6	?	Bunratty U.
Arthur	G		Tulla U.
Arthur		T	Islands
Arthur	G4	T	Tulla L.
Arthur	G	T	Bunratty L.
Atcheson	G2		Moyarta
Atkins	G		Tulla L.
Atkinson		T	Inchiquin
Austen	G	T	Moyarta
Austin	G		Islands
Austin	G		Clonderalaw
Austin	G2	T	Moyarta
Austin	G		Bunratty L.
Ayers	G		Moyarta
Ayers	G		Clonderalaw
Baggott		T	Islands
Bagot		T	Burren
Bailer	G		Moyarta
Bailey	G		Inchiquin
Bailey	G		Islands
Bailey	G		Bunratty L.
Baker	G3	T	Burren
Baker	G4	T	Bunratty U.
Baker	C2	T	Islands
Baker		T	Clonderalaw
Baker	G	T	Bunratty L.
Bakey		T	Burren
Bakay	G11	T	Corcomroe
Baldwin	G2		Tulla L.
Bales	G	T	Islands
Balcy	G		Islands
Ball	G2		Clonderalaw
Ballard		T	Islands
Ballinger	G		Burren
Ballinger		T	Corcomroe
Bollinger		T	Moyarta
Balton		T	Tulla U.
Balton	G	T	Tulla L.
Beltwin	G		Corcomroe
Banatyne	G		Inchiquin
Banatyne	G		Tulla L.
Banatyne	G		Tulla U.
Bane	G6	T	Tulla U.
Banber		T	Tulla U.
Banks		T	Islands
Bannatyne	G		Ibrickan
Bannatyne	G6		Islands
Bonnatyne	G		Bunratty U.
Barclay	G	T	Islands
Barclay	G	?	Clonderalaw
Barclay	G	T	Tulla L.
Barnett		T	Islands
Barr	G		Clonderalaw
Barret	G		Clonderalaw
Barrett	G4	T	Corcomroe
Barrett	G2	T	Inchiquin
Barrett	G2	T	Tulla U.
Barrett	G4	T	Ibrickan
Barrett	G6	T	Islands
Barrett	G		Tulla L.
Barrett	G		Moyarta
Barrett	G4	T	Clonderalaw
Barrington	G2		Corcomroe

Fig. 6.5(a). *Griffith's Valuation*: Extract from *General Index of Surnames* for the barony of Burren, Co. Clare.

SURNAME INDEX

ABBEY PARISH, BURREN BARONY, BALLYVAGHAN UNION, CO. CLARE.

Griffith's Valuation year 1855 - Tithe Applotment Book
Fiche 1.A.12   Year 1827.

Surname	G	T	Surname	G	T	Surname	G	T
Alpin	G		Hynes	G14	T	Ryder	G	
Archdeacon	G							
			Jordan	G6	T	Salmon	G	T
Bagot		T				Scott		T
Baker	G	T	Kane	G2	T	Sheehan	G	T
Beaty		T	Keating	G2	T	Skerret		T
Bindon	G2	T	Kelly	G	T	Smith	G	T
Brady	G		Kerin	G4	T	Stack	G	
Brennan	G		Kerrier		T	Sullivan		T
Browne		T	Kilkelly	G3	T			
Burke		T	King	G		Vaughan	G	
			Knee		T			
Callanan	G	T				Walsh		T
Casey	G	T	Lallie	G2		Ward		T
Clooran		T	Larkin	G	T	Whelan	G2	T
Cloughnessy	G		Lee	G	T	White	G	
Coffey	G		Leonard	G5		Wincle		T
Commons	G	T	Linnane		T			
Comyn		T	Lopham		T			
Conellan		T						
Connolly	G3	T	M'Egan	G	T			
Connors	G2		M'Guinness	G				
Cooley	G		M'Inerney	G2	T			
Cooney		T	M'Keon	G				
Coy	G		M'Mahon	G5				
Cunningham		T	M'Nally	G	T			
Curtain	G	T	M'Namara	G				
Daly	G6	T	Madden	G8	T			
Davoran	G	T	Maher	G				
Devonport	G	T	Maloney	G				
Dolan		T	Mangan	G				
Donnellan	G		Markham		T			
Donoghoe		T	Mayee		T			
Dowd	G		Mehern		T			
			Minnogue	G3	T			
Ennis	G		Molloy	G				
			Moloney	G				
Fahy	G7	T	Moran	G4	T			
Farrell	G		Moylan	G	T			
Fawl	G	T	Mulconrey	G				
Finn	G2		Mullen		T			
Fitzpatrick	G	T	Murray	G				
Flanagan	G							
Ford	G		Nee	G				
Francis		T	Nilan	G2	T			
Gavan	G		O'Brien		T			
Geoghegan		T	O'Dea	G	T			
Gorman		T	O'Pea	G				
Grady		T	O'Loughlin	G	T			
Greene	G2		O'Malley		T			
			O'Shaughnessy	G				
Halloran	G3							
Healy	G		Quealy	G				
Hehir	G	T						
Hennessy		T	Ready		T			
Higgins	G		Rice	G	T			
Hoolahan	G2	T	Roche		T			
Hoverty	G		Rorke		T			

Fig. 6.5(b). *Griffith's Valuation*: Extract from *General Index of Surnames* for the parish of Abbey, Burren Barony, Co. Clare.

PARISH OF ABBEY.

No. and Letters of Reference to Map.		Names.		Description of Tenement.	Area.		Rateable Annual Valuation.		Total Annual Valuation of Rateable Property.
		Townlands and Occupiers.	Immediate Lessors.			A. R. P.	Land. £ s. d.	Buildings. £ s. d.	£ s. d.
1		BALLYVELAGHAN *continued.*							
	b	Patrick Alpin, .	Timothy Salmon,	House, . .			—	0 9 0	0 9 0
5	a	Mrs. Mary M'Nally, {	John Bindon Scott { (*in Chancery*),	Ho. (*post office*), offs.. { and land, }	3 0 0		0 14 0	—	} 6 12 0
6					4 3 0		4 0 0	1 18 0	
	b	Michael Madden, .	Mrs. Mary M'Nally,	House, . .			—	0 2 0	0 2 0
—	—	Michael Moylan, .	Immediate Lessor.	House, . .			—	0 2 0	0 2 0
—	—			Ferry, . .			—	—	0 10 0
7	a	Catherine M'Guinness,	John Bindon Scott (*in Chancery*),	House and land, .	3 3 0		2 9 0	1 0 0	3 9 0
—	b	Bridget Connolly, .	Catherine M'Guinness,	House, . .			—	0 5 0	0 5 0
—	c	John Leonard, .	Same,	House, . .			—	0 6 0	0 6 0
—	d	Thomas Quealy, .	Rev. John Jackson,	House and garden, .	0 0 10		0 1 0	0 12 0	0 13 0
8	a	Hugh Connolly, .	John Bindon Scott { (*in Chancery*), .	House and land, .	2 1 20		{ 0 16 0	0 8 0	1 4 0
	b	Edmond Gavan,		House, office, & land,			{ 0 15 0	0 15 0	1 10 0
—	c	Patrick Connolly, .	Same, .	House and office, .			—	0 8 0	0 8 0
9	a	Thomas Hynes,	Same, {	House, office, & land, {	0 3 0		{ 0 5 0	0 10 0	0 15 0
	b	Margaret Hynes,		House and land, }			{ 0 4 0	0 14 0	0 18 0
—	c	Martin Hynes, .	Same,	House, . .			—	0 6 0	0 6 0
10		Thomas Hynes, .	Same,	Land, . .	1 1 20		0 18 0	—	0 18 0
11		Margaret Hynes,	Same,	Land, . .	1 1 20		0 18 0	—	0 18 0
12	a	John Rice, .	Same,	House and land, .	3 1 29		2 0 0	0 10 0	2 10 0
—	b	John Rice, .	John Rice, .	House, . .			—	0 5 0	0 5 0
13		Martin Hynes (*Michael*),	John Bindon Scott (*in Chancery*).	Land, . .	31 2 31		13 10 0	—	13 10 0
—	a	Michael Moylan,	Martin Hynes (*Michael*),	House and garden, .	0 1 20		0 5 0	0 3 0	0 8 0
—	b	Bridget Healy, .	Same, .	House and garden, .	0 0 15		0 1 0	0 8 0	0 9 0
—	c	Patrick Minnogue (*Jas.*)	Same,	House and garden, .	0 0 10		0 1 0	0 3 0	0 4 0
—	d	Colman Minnogue,	Same, .	House and garden, .	0 0 30		0 2 0	0 8 0	0 10 0
—	e	Michael Jordan, .	Same,	House & small garden,			—	0 10 0	0 10 0
—	f	Bridget Mangan,	Same,	House, offices, & garden,	0 0 10		0 1 0	0 10 0	0 11 0
14	a	Rev. Michael J. O'Fea,	John Bindon Scott (*in Chancery*).	Caretaker's ho., off., & ld.	23 3 13		21 0 0	24 0 0	45 0 0
—	b	John M'Keon, .	Rev. Michael J. O'Fea.	House and garden, .	0 1 20		0 7 0	1 5 0	1 12 0
—	c	Patrick Madden,	Same,	House and garden, .	0 0 30		0 3 0	0 10 0	0 13 0
—	d	Patrick Madden,	Same,	Ball-court, .			—	—	0 10 0
15		James Hynes, .	John Bindon Scott (*in Chancery*),	Land, . .	9 3 17		9 0 0	—	9 0 0
16	a	Michael Hynes, jun.,	Same,	House, offices, and land,	17 0 18		15 15 0	5 10 0	21 5 0
17	a, b			Caretaker's ho., offs., & ld.	52 0 32		50 0 0	2 15 0	52 15 0
—	c	Edmond Hoverty,	Michael Hynes, jun.,	House and garden, .	0 0 10		0 1 0	0 8 0	0 9 0
—	d	Patrick Murray,	John Bindon Scott (*in Chancery*),	House, offices, & garden,	0 0 10		0 1 0	2 0 0	2 1 0
18		Patrick Murray,	Same,	Land, . .	8 2 25		8 0 0	—	8 0 0
19		Patrick Minnogue,	Same,	House, offices, and land,	8 1 0		8 10 0	2 2 0	10 12 0
20	a	Patrick Daly, }	Same,	House, offices, & land, {	11 2 30		{ 5 10 0	1 0 0	6 10 0
		Michael Daly, }		Land, . .			{ 5 10 0	—	5 10 0
21		Patrick Daly, } Michael Daly, }	Same,	Land, . .	0 2 30		0 1 0	—	0 1 0
22	a	John Kane, .	Same,	House, offices, & land, {	0 1 10		0 1 0	—	} 12 15 0
23					10 2 35		10 0 0	2 14 0	
24	a	Patrick Madden (*Denis*),	Same,	House, offices, and land,	6 3 38		6 0 0	1 10 0	7 10 0
25	a	Michael Hynes, sen.,	Same,	House, offices, and land,	6 1 20		5 10 0	2 5 0	7 15 0
26				Water and waste, .	15 2 32		—	—	—
27	a	John M'Mahon,	John Bindon Scott (*in Chancery*),	House, offices, and land,	26 2 24		21 10 0	2 16 0	24 6 0
28		John M'Mahon,	Same,	Land, . .	39 3 12		14 0 0	—	14 0 0
—	a	Denis Brennan, .	John M'Mahon,	House & small garden, .			—	0 5 0	0 5 0
29		Michael Molloy,	John Bindon Scott (*in Chancery*),	Garden, . .	0 1 30		0 2 0	—	0 2 0
30		William J. Skerrett,	Same,	Land, . .	4 2 25		4 10 0	—	4 10 0
31		Rev. James Coffey,	William J. Skerrett,	Land, . .	0 3 20		0 17 0	—	0 17 0
32	a	Margaret Cloughessy,	Same,	House and land, .	1 0 28		1 5 0	0 9 0	1 12 0
—	b	Rev. James Coffey,	Margaret Cloughessy,	House, office, & garden,			—	1 0 0	1 1 0
33		Rev. James Coffey,	Same,	Land, . .	2 3 7		2 14 0	—	2 14 0
				Total, .	311 3 16		221 19 0	67 11 0	290 10 0
				EXEMPTIONS:					
2	b	Rev. John Jackson,	John Finn,	Church and yard, .	0 2 20		—	1 10 0	1 10 0
				Total, exclusive of Exemptions, ..	311 0 36		221 19 0	66 1 0	289 0 0

Fig. 6.6. *Griffith's Valuation*: Corresponding entry on valuation document.

not shown in the index. When searching for a parish, you should bear in mind the following points:

(a) the parishes referred to are Civil and not ecclesiastical although their boundaries tend to coincide with parishes of the Church of Ireland. They do not coincide with boundaries of the Roman Catholic Church, and

(b) care should be taken to ascertain in which Poor Law Union(s) a parish is situated, some parishes being 'shared' by more than one Union.

Thus some Roman Catholic and Church of Ireland parishes appear in more than one Union, causing many family historians to complete a parish search, unaware that part of that parish lies in an adjoining Union a few pages away. The value of the *Townland Index* (described in Chapter 1) now becomes obvious, for in addition to its other benefits, it also lists the Union(s) in which 'civil' parishes lie. *Griffith's Valuation* may prove difficult to use for the first time, but this information will help to overcome some of those difficulties.

The microfiche version

Griffith's Valuation is also available on microfiche, small photographic cards that are viewed on special machines called 'viewers'. The microfiche are produced by Irish Microforms Ltd., Dublin, in eight small boxes, two of which contain the National Library's *General Index of Surnames.* They are described more fully in another book currently being written by the author.

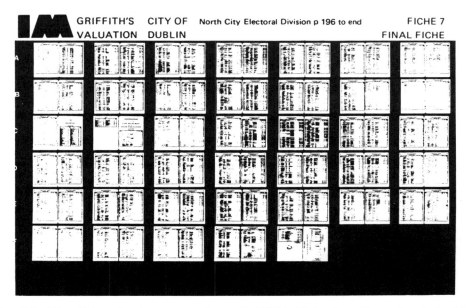

Fig. 6.7. Microfiche showing a pag from *Griffith's Valuation*. (Reproduced by kind permission of Irish Microforms Ltd., Dublin.

A note of warning
Griffith's Valuation was not intended to be a census, and therefore does not show everybody living in a particular area. During and after the famine, many people became landless or homeless and were therefore not recorded by the survey. The occupants of Dublin tenements were not recorded either.

Sources
Griffith's Valuation can be seen at The National Archives (NA), Dublin, The National Library of Ireland (NLI), Dublin, and The Public Record Office of Northern Ireland (PRONI), Belfast. County libraries and heritage centres around Ireland have full collections or extracts relating to their county (see Appendix A).

Alternative sources
The British Library (BL) in London have the full collection on microfiche and some printed volumes covering a number of counties. Also in London, the Irish Genealogical Research Society (IGRS) possesses a complete collection on microfiche and a few counties are retained in the Society of Genealogists' (SOG) library

Notebooks and other records
Notebooks were used by valuers during the survey and many of those covering Southern Ireland will be found in the NA and Valuation Office, Dublin. Those for Northern Ireland are in the PRONI. *Griffith's Valuation* has been regularly revised since the original survey and books showing successive changes in landholding up to the present day can also be seen in the Valuation Office (see Chapter 5).

Land Valuation documents

When Sir. Richard Griffith began his work, his intention was to survey all land and property in Ireland for the purpose of taxation. The results, popularly known as *Griffith's Valuation* (see that title), are described elsewhere in this chapter. During the survey, which took 19 years to complete, notebooks were carried by survey teams in which to record details of property and its owners/occupiers. This information was used to compile the *Primary Valuation of Tenements* (*Griffth's Valuation*).

The Valuation Office in Dublin, kept a record of all changes in circumstances, for example, when land changed hands through death, sale or gift, which was noted in manuscript books together with the date the change occurred. Many of the changes were also noted on ordnance survey maps. When the manuscript books became too cluttered, new ones were brought into use and filed with the old 'cancelled' books. From these, it is possible to trace the ownership of a piece of land up to the present day.

Sources

Surveyors' cancelled and current land books plus related maps will be found in the Valuation Office, Dublin. Field, House and Tenure books for the Republic of Ireland are available in the National Archives. Similar documents relating to Northern Ireland will be found in the Public Record Office of Northern Ireland.

The tithe applotment survey

Tithes were taxes paid by occupiers of agricultural land for the upkeep of the Anglican

Diocese of *Achonry*   Parish of *Kilfree*

TOWNLAND.	NAMES OF OCCUPIERS.	TITHEABLE.					
		Quantities in Detail.	Quality.	Total Quantity in Holding.	Total Quantity in Townland.	Rents paid.	Real Acreable Value.
33 *...gnole Town continued*	Thomas Taylor	" " 27	Plots Good	" " 27	" " "	2 15 4¾	4 " "
4	John Clements	" 3 6	D⁰	" 3 6	" " "		4 " "
5	Shady Lavin	" 3 33	D⁰	" 3 33	" " "		4 " "
6	William Ross	" " 32	D⁰	" " 32	" " "		4 " "
7	John Davis	" " 16	D⁰	" " 16	" " "		4 " "
8	Edward Sands	" " 21	D⁰	" " 21	" " "		4 " "
9	Tho⁵ Donagha	" 1 9	D⁰	" 1 9	" " "	3 13 10½	4 " "
40	Sir Robt B. Gore Bart	" 2 "	D⁰	" 2 "	" " "		4 " "
1	Tho⁵ Durkin	" " 19	D⁰	" " 19	" " "	2 15 4	4 " "
2	Sir Robt B. Gore Bart	" 2 7	D⁰	" 2 7	" " "		4 " "
3	John Coaghlan	" " 34	D⁰	" " 34	" " "		4 " "
4	Sir Robt B. Gore Bart	" 2 3	D⁰	" 2 3	" " "		4 " "
5	Patt Beereen	" " 30	D⁰	" " 30	" " "	1 16 11	4 " "
6	John Armstrong	" " 31	D⁰	" " 31	" " "		4 " "
	Mr Whittaker	" 1 33	D⁰	" " "	" " "	30 0 0	16 " "
7	Mr Whittaker	" " 30	Garden	" " "	" " "	6 0 0	4 " "
8	Mr Whittaker	6 " 12	arable	6 2 35	" " "	19 14 0	2 4 "
9	Joseph Langhead	" 1 "	Plot	" 1 "	" " "	4 0 0	16 " "
50	Mary Dyer	" " 11	D⁰	" " 11	" " "		16 " "
1	John Motherwell Esq	" " 11	D⁰	" " 11	" " "		16 " "
2	James O'Beirne	" " 9	D⁰	" " 9	" " "		16 " "
3	John Feighney	" " 17	D⁰	" " 17	" " "		16 " "
4	Mr Motherwell	" " 17	D⁰	" " 17	" " "		16 " "
5	Robt Morrison	" " 12	D⁰	" " 12	" " "		16 " "
6	John Motherwell	" " 32	Potts garden	" " 32	" " "		16 " "
7	Edwd O'Brien	" " 16	Plot	" " 16	" " "	2 15 4	16 " "
8	Tho⁵ Durkin	" " 4	D⁰	" " 4	" " "	2 16 10	20 " "
9	Bartly Herins	" " 16	D⁰	" " 16	" " "	2 15 4	20 " "
60	Widow McGetrick	" " 16	D⁰	" " 16	" " "	3 0 0	16 " "
1	Tho⁵ Durkin	" " 9	D⁰	" " 9	" " "		16 " "
2	Bartly Herins	" 1 16	Garden	" 1 16	" " "	18 4½	2 4 "
3	Widow McGetrick	" 1 16	D⁰	" 1 16	" " "	18 4½	2 4 "

Fig. 6.8. Extract from Co. Sligo *Tithe Applotment Book.*

(Protestant) Church of Ireland. From the reign of Elizabeth I, tithes were also payable by the Roman Catholic population, leading to disturbances resulting in deaths and injuries. Previously paid in kind, i.e. agricultural produce or livestock, the change to payment in cash required a survey and valuation of agricultural land. The result, the tithe applotments compiled between 1828 and 1837, are arranged in separate volumes for each parish. These show occupiers' names, quantity of land and amounts to be paid. They do not list families or landless persons. The survey did not include non-agricultural land. Researchers may find a small number of parishes missing or displaying a certificate showing an overall valuation.

The indexes

The National Library's *General Index of Surnames,* described in the section on *Griffith's Valuation,* also includes surnames contained in the Tithe Applotment Books, such names being indicated by T for Tithe but for some unknown reason, their frequency is not shown.

Sources

Tithe Applotment Books for the Republic of Ireland will be found in the National Archives, Dublin, where there are also copies of the Northern Ireland books. Tithes for Northern Ireland will be found in the Public Record Office of Northern Ireland (PRONI) Belfast who also have copies of the Tithe Applotments for most of Cavan, Donegal and Monaghan. The Irish Genealogical Research Society (IGRS) in London, also has a collection of tithes for Northern Ireland on microfiche.

The Tithe Applotments have been published on microfiche by Irish Microforms Ltd., Dublin.

The 1873 Return of Owners of Land

Following a debate in the House of Lords, a survey in 1873 revealed there were 301,000 landowners in the United Kingdom. The survey, nicknamed the *New Domesday* was published in 1876 and officially known as *The Return of Owners of Land.* These lists, arranged by county, show in alphabetical order, landowners (not tenants) possessing one acre or more, in England, Wales, Scotland and Ireland. The returns for each county in Ireland show (a) the recorded population during the 1871 census, (b) the number of inhabited houses, (c) landowners' names arranged in alphabetical order, (d) their address, which may be elsewhere in the United Kingdom, and (e) the extent and valuation of their land.

The returns include further alphabetical lists, arranged by acreage, e.g. "20,000 acres and upwards", "20,000 to 10,000 acres", etc. These show (a) proprietors' names and titles and (b) the extent and annual valuation of the land.

Sources

The returns for Ireland will be found in the NA, PRONI, and local sources around the country.

An alternative source

The British Library and PRO in London also hold returns for England, Scotland, Wales and Ireland which will be found in the *British Parliamentary Papers* (see this chapter). The returns for Ireland have been republished by the Genealogical Publishing Company, Baltimore.

QUEEN'S COUNTY.

Population in 1871, . . 79,771.

Inhabited Houses, . . 15,519.

Name of Owner.	Address of Owner.	Extent.			Valuation.		Name of Owner.	Address of Owner.	Extent.		
		A.	R.	P.	£	s.			A.	R.	P.
Adair, John G., . .	Rathdair, Monaster-evan.	9,655	1	20	3,719	15	Bray, Rev. James, .	Rathtillig, . . .	16	2	30
							Brennan, John, . .	Leagh, . . .	47	1	20
Alley, George, .	Donaghmore, Ossory, .	176	0	10	124	0	Brennan, Patrick, .	Kilkenny, . . .	112	0	10
Alloway, Robert M., .	Ballyshanduffe, Bally-brittas.	366	1	10	155	0	Brennan, Thomas, .	Monavea, . . .	16	1	30
							Brennan, Thomas, .	Strahard, Mountmelick,	1	2	20
Anderson, William, .	Clonminau, Mary-borough.	20	0	0	12	0	Brennan, William, .	Eglish, Rathdowney, .	49	0	0
							Bridge, Rev. Frederick,		8	1	30
Annesley, Earl of, .	Castlewellan, co. Down,	2,489	2	25	1,606	5	Bridge, Timothy, Reps. of.	Millpark, Rosina, .	1	3	35
Armstrong, Harvey, .	Rathleash, Portarling-ton.	46	0	30	46	10					
Ashbrook, Viscount, .	The Castle, Durrow, .	4,515	2	20	3,412	15	Brooks, Richard N., .	Castle Howard, co. Wicklow.	1,096	3	20
Aspa, Mrs. Adelaide, .	11, Grantham-street, Dublin.	124	0	0	68	15	Broomfield, George, .	Harristown, Rath-downey.	259	0	30
Atkinson, Samuel, .	Ardough, . . .	54	3	30	15	5	Brown, Francis D., .	Coolmoney, Stafford-on-Slaney, co. Wicklow.	1,493	0	15
Ayres, Rev. George, .	Blessington, . .	616	1	15	455	15	Brown, Rev. J., .	Kelvin Grove, co. Carlow,	665	1	10
							Brown, Samuel, .	Mountmelick, .	5	2	30
							Browne, Robert C., .	Browne's Hill, .	163	1	20
							Burke, Patrick, .	Graigue, . .	8	1	0
							Burrowes, Peter .	86, Lower Gardiner-st, Dublin.	61	2	25
Bailey, Daniel, Reps. of,	Morrock, Moate, .	230	3	20	51	10	Burton, W. F., .	Burton Hall, county, Carlow.	155	3	30
Bailey, John T., .	Thumfarin, Vicarstown, Stradbally.	10	2	30	9	10					
Bailey, Thomas A., .	Bellvue, Castledermott,	893	0	0	499	10	Butler, Edward F., .	—	1,077	3	10
Bank, of Ireland, .	Maryborough, . .	1	2	30	38	10	Butler, Hon. Maria T., .	—	290	1	35
Bank, National, .	Mountmelick, . .	3	0	5	54	0	Butler, Paget, .	—	78	2	30
Banks, James, .	166, Townsend-street, Dublin.	20	2	20	28	5	Butler, Pierce, .	Kilkenny, . .	842	2	15
							Butler, Robert, Reps. of,	Dublin, . .	448	3	35
Banks, John, Reps. of, .	Rockview, Borris-in-Ossory.	58	1	0	58	10	Byrne, Matthew, .	Carlow, . .	111	0	35
							Byrne, Richard, .	Graigue, Mountmelick,	312	1	35
Barrow Navigation Co.,		152	2	10	199	5					
Barton, William, .	Ballinfrase, Rath-downey.	292	3	10	189	5					
Baxter, Mrs. Frances H.,	Ashbank House, Blair-gowrie, Scotland.	625	0	0	321	10	Campion, Susan, .	—	57	1	20
							Canal Compy., (Grand),	Dublin, . .	285	3	15
Beamish, J. N., . .	Queenstown, Cork, .	89	3	20	62	0	Candle, William, .	Malahide, . .	87	3	2
Bell, Wellington, Reps. of.	Timahoe, Abbeyleix, .	65	1	10	99	5	Carbery, Lord, Reps. of,	The Castle, Cork, .	2,919	3	15
							Garden, Major Henry D.,	Knightstown, Portar-lington.	2,225	2	30
Bellew, Mrs. Grattan,	Mount Bellew, co. Gal-way.	10,593	3	25	5,923	10	Carew, Lord, .	Castleborough, Ennis-corthy.	1,098	2	30
Bergan, Edward, .	Monavea, . . .	10	0	20	3	0					
Birch, Rev. John, .	Borris-in-Ossory, .	113	1	35	122	15	Carey, Pierce, Reps. of,	Stanney, . .	110	2	30
Bland, John Loftus, .	Blandsfort, Abbeyleix,	978	0	0	634	0	Carey, Thomas, .	—	29	3	5
Bolton, William, .	Athanilla, Mountrath,	85	3	20	42	10	Carroll, Anne, .	Ballybrittas, Portar-lington.	1	1	0
Bond, William S., .	Agent—Frederick Guest, Athy.	92	0	0	59	0					
Booth, Juliana, .	Lansdowne, Crescent, Bath.	1,252	2	20	693	10	Carter, John, .	—	555	3	10
							Carter, Samuel R., .	Monavea, . .	845	1	15
Booth, Robert, .	Carlow, . . .	6	1	20	8	5	Carter, Willoughby H.,	—	95	3	25
Barrowes, Sir Erasmus D., bart.	Barnetstown Castle, Ballymore-Eustace.	2,467	1	35	1,254	5	Cassan, Joseph, .	Ballyknocken, Mary-borough.	124	0	5
Barrowes, Samuel, Reps. of.	5, Alma-terrace, Monks-town, co. Dublin.	4	3	35	30	0	Cassan, Matthew, .	America, . .	22	0	5
							Cassan, Matthew, S., .	Sheffield, Maryborough,	1,979	0	10
Barrowes, Captain Wal-ter.	Portarlington, . .	7	0	30	8	10	Cassidy, James, .	Monasterevan, .	376	1	0
							Cassin, Patrick, .	Knockhed, . .	10	0	35
Bowen, Captain Charles H.	Kilnacourt, Portarling-ton, and 13, Longford-terrace, Monkstown.	2,120	1	0	1,324	0	Castletown, The Right Hon. Lord.	Lisduff, Errill, Temple-more.	22,241	1	0
							Caulfield, Edmund, .	—	348	2	20
Bradish, James, .	Enniscorthy, . .	84	0	5	72	10	Champ, Arthur, .	Ballymorris, Portar-lington.	2	0	5
Bradley, Edward, .	Barradoos, Clonaslee, .	415	1	20	42	5					
Bradley, Thomas, .	—	7	0	20	17	5	Champ, Benjamin, .	Ballymorris, Portar-lington.	4	1	0
Brady, John B., .	Myshall, Carlow, .	207	0	15	124	10	Champ, Isaac, .	Coolegeggan, Rathan-gan.	47	3	0
Brandon, Rev. William,	—	4	1	30	6	5					

L :

Fig. 6.9(a). Extract from *Owners of Land 1876 (Ireland)* relating to Queen's County.

COUNTY OF CLARE.

PROPRIETORS.	Area.	Annual Valuation.	PROPRIETORS.	Area.	Annual Valuation.
20,000 Acres and upwards.	Statute Acres.	£.	**5,000 to 2,000 Acres—continued.**	Statute Acres.	£.
?egham, Marquess of	24,059	9,704	Fitzgerald, Right Honourable J. D.	2,003	913
?quin, Lord	21,178	11,077	Fitzgerald, John Foster V.	2,531	721
?field, Lord	59,048	16,558	Fitzgerald, George F.	2,060	185
?by, Ed. P.	27,289	7,881	Fitzgerald, William F. V.	3,708	895
			Griffith, Richard, jun.	4,957	1,132
			Hickman, Colonel	2,772	1,591
20,000 to 10,000 Acres.			Hickman, Hugh P.	3,191	1,486
?ly, Lord	19,266	6,218	Joly, Jasper	2,421	665
?r, Reps. of James	11,727	3,794	Keane, Marcus	4,563	1,353
?erald, Sir Augustine, bart.	14,275	6,017	Limerick, Earl of	2,565	1,069
?amara, Colonel Francis	14,063	6,484	Lloyd, Reps. Thomas	2,335	1,147
?ren, Henry D. Stafford	12,761	6,696	Lynch, John Wilson	3,098	1,042
?kleur, Colonel C. M.	19,757	9,389	M'Mahon, Timothy	2,303	201
			M'Mahon, Sir Beresford, bart.	4,662	1,737
			Mahon, Charles G.	2,303	410
10,000 to 5,000 Acres.			Mahon, Reps. Charles	2,336	1,328
?ar, Thomas	9,764	3,567	Martin, John G.	2,025	509
?tae, Wyndham	6,768	2,390	Martin, Nicholas	2,220	351
?m, Francis N.	7,317	2,805	Molony, Crossdale	2,181	951
?, Austin	7,358	2,262	Molony, Henry G.	4,659	358
?b, Cornelius	5,736	2,569	Norbury, Earl of	2,461	782
?t, Thomas	8,769	3,614	O'Callaghan, John	4,483	1,596
?cue, Pierce	5,278	1,341	O'Callaghan, Reps. Henry	2,124	273
?rald, William	9,730	3,885	O'Connell, Trustees of Eliza	4,740	1,287
?, Ed. Arthur	8,562	3,357	Patterson, Marcus	2,991	592
?, Thomas R.	7,830	2,136	Quin, Lord George	2,858	2,000
?, Matthew	5,699	955	Reeves, Robert William E.	2,180	1,307
?nell, William E. A.	6,754	2,488	Sampson, George	3,246	884
?th, William H.	5,547	1,953	Scott, John	4,305	1,610
?, Sir Hugh D., bart.	5,031	3,669	Skerritt, William J.	2,466	1,207
?y, William Mills	9,892	2,550	Smith, Edward V., and Mrs. Fallon	2,503	759
?nd, William J. H.	5,144	1,646	Stacpoole, Jane	2,678	1,146
?n, James	5,336	1,724	Stratford, John W.	2,220	913
?u, Reps. William J.	6,440	794	Studdert, Rev. George	2,235	815
?gham, Captain Charles George	8,823	3,718	Studdert, Richard	2,759	512
?gton, Colonel E. F. H.	5,584	1,543	Studdert, Thomas	4,832	2,646
?, Hon. Louisa	6,305	2,567	Synge, Francis H.	2,967	1,261
?ole, Richard	7,920	3,035	Synge, Geo. Charles	2,948	205
?ole, William	7,370	3,383	Timmons, James	2,614	1,096
?on, Donat	8,167	776	Westropp, John	2,937	1,738
?t, John V.	6,726	1,627	Westropp, Ralph	4,332	1,803
			Whitlock, George	2,672	425
5,000 to 2,000 Acres.			**2,000 to 1,000 Acres.**		
?rong, Ed. A.	3,151	2,141	Bagot, John J.	1,073	69
?r Colonel Thomas	2,252	725	Barclay, George	1,715	524
Hon. Julia	3,184	2,622	Bentick, A. H. F. C.	1,509	347
?, Bagot	4,758	760	Bentley, William	1,100	331
?, William B.	2,177	500	Blackburne, Captain F.	1,234	587
?er, John	2,559	916	Blood, E. D.	1,078	303
?t, Reps. William	3,105	586	Blood, E. M.	1,441	929
?, William	2,306	449	Blood, Millicent	1,204	337
?dan, Frederick M.	4,310	970	Bolton, Charles P.	1,453	532
?, Pierce	2,342	632	Borough, Robert H.	1,279	676
?, Wainwright	3,277	1,704	Brady, J. Beauchamp	1,664	667
?in, Francis	2,123	521	Brew, William	1,672	521
?, Richard	3,038	465	Brooke, Sir A. bart., and Lady Franklin	1,293	672
?ere, Henry V.	3,278	1,975	Butler, Henry	1,394	417
?rigo, Duchess	2,221	955	Carroll, John	1,493	902
			Clarke, Hon. C. B., and S. Wandesforde	1,716	501
			Cullinan, Michael	1,763	560

Fig. 6.9(b). Extract from *Owners of Land 1876 (Ireland)* relating to Co. Clare.

Parish records

Parish records suffered from the ravages of history and the questions most commonly asked today are: "What registers survive?" and "Where can they be found?" Some facts will clarify the position.

Church of Ireland parish registers

In 1560, the Anglican Church became the established church in Ireland with Queen Elizabeth I of England as its head. Other religions in Ireland were 'tolerated', with the exception of Roman Catholics and to a lesser degree, Presbyterians, who were also subjected to the harshness of Penal Laws.

Sources

The majority of Church of Ireland registers commence between the late 1700s and early 1800s although some began as early as the mid-1600s. In 1876, the law required Church of Ireland registers to be deposited in the Four Courts building in Dublin. Most of these were deposited and subsequently destroyed in 1922. Others, including those not sent to Dublin have survived and remain today with local clergy or the Representative Church Body Library (RCBL) in Dublin. The National Archives (NA) have some originals and copies of many others. The Public Record Office of Northern Ireland (PRONI) have copies of many registers relating to Northern Ireland.

Roman Catholic parish registers

After the Anglican Church became the established Church of Ireland, Roman Catholic influence waned although most of the population remained Catholic. As a result, the preservation of Roman Catholic records suffered. From 1869, when the Church of Ireland was disestablished, the Roman Catholic Church once again became dominant, reorganising itself and its records.

Sources

Because Roman Catholic registers were excluded from the 1876 requirement (see Church of Ireland parish registers), they remained with local parishes and largely escaped destruction, many still remaining in those parishes today. Few records of this nature survive before the 1750s, the majority commencing in the early or late 1800s. Parish records in cities and large towns generally begin earlier than those in country areas.

The National Library of Ireland (NLI) has microfilmed copies of most Roman Catholic registers of which many are available for examination. Some dioceses are reluctant for their copies to be examined unless permission from the relevant parish priest has been obtained in writing. The PRONI have copies of registers relating to Northern Ireland. Enquiries concerning availability should be addressed to the NLI, RCBL or PRONI enclosing an SAE. (See also Chapter 2.)

Presbyterian church records

By 1603, many Presbyterians from Scotland and England had settled in Ulster where they too suffered persecution for their beliefs. During the early years of persecution, Presbyterians were required to attend services in the Anglican church. Prior to the late 18th century, their marriages were declared illegal unless conducted in the established church.

Surviving Presbyterian registers are kept locally by (a) Presbyterian ministers, (b) the Presbyterian Historical Society, and (c) PRONI who are currently in the process of copying all surviving Presbyterian registers. The NA has copies of most registers kept by local clergy in Northern Ireland, and a list of many records in the Presbyterian Historical Society. A result of the earlier persecutions is that some events, (particularly those of earlier years) will be found in the registers of the (Anglican) Church of Ireland.

The Religious Society of Friends (Quakers)

The Society of Friends were a religious sect from England that settled in Ireland during the Cromwellian era. They are now credited with having some of the best-kept religious records in the world.

Sources

Dating mainly from 1671 (some began in 1667), Quaker records consisting of births, marriages, deaths, burials and other material will be found in the libraries of the Society of Friends in Dublin and Lisburn. The Society of Friends in Dublin welcomes enquiries from the public who are permitted to visit during opening times. No fee is charged for consulting records but donations are welcomed. The Society's Library in Lisburn is only available for postal enquiries. Certain Quaker records will also be found in the PRONI.

Census substitutes

There exists in Ireland and elsewhere large quantities of material that may be used as substitutes for records that were destroyed. Commonly known as census substitutes, they include surveys and local censuses compiled for a variety of purposes, and directories covering many cities and towns. Originals and copies will be found in the National Archives and other sources around Ireland. They are described in greater detail by Rosemary ffolliott in *Irish Genealogy: A Record Finder.*

A 'modern' substitute

A more recent substitute is now available worldwide. As part of their international project, the Church of Jesus Christ of Latter-Day Saints, commonly known as the Mormon Church, have extracted millions of names from parish registers, census returns and other records around the world. These extracts, arranged alphabetically within each country, are indexed in the *International Genealogical Index* (IGI); a series of microfiche containing, in the 1992 edition, approximately 187 million entries, of which nearly two million relate to Ireland. The IGI is useful to family historians by (a) showing extracts from material otherwise inaccessible to family historians, (b) identifying sources from which entries were taken (the codes in the right-hand columns), and (c) enabling family historians to obtain, at minimal cost, a copy of the original record from which such entries were taken.

Many of the entries, some dating from the 1700s, will help those who wish to progress beyond the start of Irish civil registration. Microfiche relating to countries that were subject to immigration, include details of Irish immigrants and their descendants.

Caution

The IGI is an excellent guide to the existence of original material but it is first and foremost an index, drawing attention to material existing elsewhere; code numbers in the

DAVIS, JAMES

COUNTRY: IRELAND | COUNTY: IRELAND | AS OF MAR 1988 | PAGE 6,448

NAME	SEX: M MALE/F FEMALE/H HUSBAND/W WIFE — FATHER/MOTHER OR SPOUSE	SEX	TYPE	EVENT DATE	COUNTY, TOWN, PARISH	B	E	S	SOURCE BATCH	SOURCE SERIAL SHEET
DAVIS, JAMES	CHARLOTTE COLLINS	H	M	1807	QUEENS,DURROW			19JAN1977LA	M701011	0091
DAVIES, JAMES	LOUISA DAVIES	H	M	24SEP1816	CORK,RATHCOONEY			08JAN1970OK	A538011	1301
DAVIS, JAMES	ROBERT DAVIS/JANE	M	C	14JUN1818	DOWN,KNOCKBREDA	11MAR1975OG	10APR1975OG	18JUN1975OG	7415510	22
DAVIS, JAMES	JAMES DAVIS/HARIOT	M	C	NOV1825	MONAGHAN,CLONES	14OCT1976PV	21DEC1976PV	13JAN1977PV	C700681	7170
DAVIS, JAMES	MARTHA GRAY	H	M	09JAN1833	ANTRIM,AGHALEE			14JUN1976SL	M700141	0349
DAVIS, JAMES	WILLIAM DAVIS/MARGARET HASLOPP	M	B	10APR1833	DOWN,DROMARA,PRESBYTERIAN	11APR1975PV	16MAY1975PV	10JUN1975PV	C700041	1452
DAVIS, JAMES	MATHW DAVIS/ANNE MC GUADE	M	C	15OCT1833	MONAGHAN,CLONES	14OCT1976PV	18DEC1976PV	15JAN1977PV	C700681	9079
DAVY, JAMES	JOHN DAVY/JANE FITZSIMONS	M	B	28APR1835	DOWN,BOARDMILLS,PRESBYTERIAN	10APR1975PV	14MAY1975PV	06JUN1975PV	C700011	1535
DAVIS, JAMES	JOE DAVIS/JANE	M	C	20MAY1838	TIPPERARY,MODREENY	12MAR1977OG	28APR1977OG	21JUL1977OG	C701021	0352
DAVIS, JAMES	WILLIAM DAVIS/MARY WILSON	M	B	19JAN1840	ANTRIM,BELFAST	07MAY1971MT	18AUG1971MT	03FEB1972MT	7026409	94
DAVIS, JAMES	ELIZABETH ROGERS	H	M	13JAN1846	DONEGAL,KILLAGHTEE			17MAY1973OK	7226215	7
DAVIS, JAMES	MARIA LAWLESS	H	M	14MAR1846	DUBLIN,DUBLIN,ST PETER			17MAY1973OK	7226215	9
DAVIES, JAMES	ISABELLA NEWPORT	H	M	21APR1846	WATERFORD,WATERFORD,0627			15APR1987LA	M701741	0595
DAVIS, JAMES	JAMES DAVIS/EMELIA BANN	M	B	23APR1846	DOWN,MOIRA	14MAY1975PV	24JUN1975PV	15JUL1975PV	C700401	1059
DAVIS, JAMES	ELIZABETH SCOTT	H	M	30JUL1846	WEXFORD,BALLYHUSKARD			17MAY1973OK	7226215	10
DAVIS, JAMES	CHARLOTTE SMITH	H	M	02NOV1846	DUBLIN,DUBLIN,ST BRIDGET			17MAY1973OK	7226215	26
DAVIS, JAMES	ELEANOR BURDON	H	M	26NOV1848	DOWN,DRUMGOOLAND			17MAY1973OK	7226215	21
DAVIS, JAMES	CATHERINE DALY	H	M	27APR1851	DUBLIN,DUBLIN,ST MARYS			09FEB1973PV	7211031	10
DAVIS, JAMES	JAMES DAVIS/MARGARET HUEY	M	B	30SEP1851	TYRONE,BRIGH,PRESBYTERIAN	14MAR1975MT	17APR1975MT	20MAY1975MT	C700191	0290
DAVIS, JAMES	WILLIAM DAVIS/CHARLOTTE	M	C	25MAY1852	DOWN,KILLANEY PARISH,PRESBYTERIAN	12APR1975PV	20MAY1975PV	13JUN1975PV	C700091	0084
DAVIES, JAMES	PAT DAVIES/BRIDGET KELLY OR LYONS	M	B	12FEB1864	GALWAY,MOUNT BELLEW,0364	07JUN1986SE	31JUL1986SE	01AUG1986SE	C701224	3210
DAVIS, JAMES	ANDREW DAVIS/CLARINNA DELAP	M	B	22FEB1864	DONEGAL,KILLYBEGS,0123	04MAR1987JR	26MAR1987JR	01APR1987JR	C701227	1060
DAVIS, JAMES	MICHAEL DAVIS/MARGARET RING	M	B	28APR1864	WATERFORD,LISMORE DISTRICT,0820	12JUN1986JR	15JUL1986JR	25JUL1986JR	C701229	7380
DAVY, JAMES	ANDREW DAVY/ROSE BYRNE	M	B	31MAY1864	WESTMEATH,MILLTOWN DISTRICT,0334	17FEB1984OG	04APR1984OG	02MAY1984OG	C701234	2891
DAVIS, JAMES	WILLIAM DAVIS/JULIA MURRAY	M	B	19JUL1864	DUBLIN,STILLORGAN,0926	09APR1985JR	08MAY1986JR	21MAY1986JR	C701233	8254
DAVIS, JAMES	PETER DAVIS/MARY DONOHOE	M	B	01AUG1864	ROSCOMMON,BALLYLEAGUE DISTRICT,0357	14JAN1986JR	08FEB1986JR	25FEB1986JR	C701239	3077
DAVIES, JAMES	THOMAS DAVIES/ISABELLA DONNELLY	M	B	27DEC1864	DOWN,BALLYMACARRET,0384	12DEC1985BO	01FEB1986BO	05FEB1986BO	C701251	3818
DAVYS, JAMES	JAMES DAVYS/ELLEN CRYAN	M	B	23JAN1865	SLIGO,BALLYMOTE,0372	20SEP1986JR	24OCT1986JR	05NOV1986JR	C701252	3098
DAVY, JAMES	PATRICK DAVY/MARY BOURKE	M	B	22MAR1865	TIPPERARY,MOYNE,0719	21JUN1984SL	30AUG1984SL	05SEP1984SL	C701253	6326
DEEVEY, JAMES	JAMES DEEVEY/ANN BOYCE	M	B	30MAR1865	WICKLOW,BLESSINGTON,0927	28FEB1987JR	24MAR1987JR	31MAR1987JR	C701257	8543
DAVIS, JAMES	THOMAS DAVIS/SUBINA CONNOR	M	B	23MAY1865	KINGS,TULLAMORE,0828	04JUN1986OG	16AUG1986OG	04SEP1986OG	C701258	7164
DAVIS, JAMES	JAMES DAVIS/MARGARET OBEIRNE	M	B	26MAY1865	SLIGO,CARNEY,0349	CLEARED	CLEARED	CLEARED	C701257	3190
DAVEY, JAMES	MICHAEL DAVEY/BRIDGET WALSH	M	B	09AUG1865	SLIGO,SLIGO,0341	28NOV1986OG	12FEB1987OG	17FEB1987OG	C701263	2979
DAVIS, JAMES	ANTHONY DAVIS/ELIZABETH TREMBLE	M	B	19SEP1865	MAYO,CROSSMOLINA,0015	31MAY1986OK	08JUL1986OK	29AUG1986OK	C701271	0132
DAVIS, JAMES	THOMAS DAVIS/ANNE CONOLLY	M	B	23NOV1865	DONEGAL,KILLYBEGS,0124	18FEB1986JR	12MAR1986JR	29MAR1986JR	C701268	1122
DAVIS, JAMES	WILLIAM DAVIS/MARY DONLON	M	B	25NOV1865	GALWAY,AHASCRAGH,0022	31MAY1986OK	08JUL1986OK	29AUG1986OK	C701271	0196
DEEVY, JAMES	EDWARD DEEVY/MARY FLOOD	M	B	09JAN1866	KILKENNY,CASTLECOMER,0555	21FEB1986PV	06MAR1986PV	15MAR1986PV	C701283	5042
DAVIS, JAMES	JAMES DAVIS/ANNE ORR	M	B	22APR1866	DONEGAL,RATHMELTON,0251	CLEARED	CLEARED	CLEARED	C701293	2176
DAVIS, JAMES	THOMAS DAVIS/NANNE FULLER	M	B	11MAY1866	KERRY,LISTOWEL,0501	28JUN1985OG	08OCT1985OG	13NOV1985OG	C701291	4675
DAVIS, JAMES	MARGARET RYAN	H	M	25MAY1866	LIMERICK,LIMERICK,ST MICHAELS			01MAY1974AL	7306109	13
DEVEY, JAMES	JAMES DEVEY/ANNE ROACHE	M	B	04JUN1866	KINGS,TULLAMORE,0789	14JUN1986LA	16JUL1986LA	18JUL1986LA	C701288	6890
DEVOY, JAMES	JAMES DEVOY/MARY MURPHY	M	B	10JUL1866	DUBLIN,DUBLIN,0669	CLEARED	CLEARED	CLEARED	C701293	5926
DAVEY, JAMES	HUGH DAVEY/ELIZA ROBINSON	M	B	11JUL1866	DOWN,BALLYNAHINCH,0517	24MAY1986OK	26JUN1986OK	22AUG1986OK	C701292	4743
DAVIS, JAMES	PATRICK DAVIS/MARY DOHENY	M	B	14JUL1866	CLARE,ANNACARRIGA,0459	11MAR1986JR	09APR1986JR	15APR1986JR	C701295	4191
DAVIS, JAMES	THOMAS DAVIS/MARGARET BYRNES	M	B	09SEP1866	WATERFORD,TALLOW,0776	13MAR1986JR	10APR1986JR	17APR1986JR	C701295	7064
DAVEY, JAMES	JOHN DAVEY/CATHERINE CAMPBELL	M	B	19SEP1866	DOWN,BALLYNAHINCH,0484	CLEARED	CLEARED	CLEARED	C701297	4490
DAVEY, JAMES	JOHN DAVEY/ELIZA MCMEEKIN	M	B	02DEC1866	ANTRIM,BALLYCARRY,0582	CLEARED	CLEARED	CLEARED	C701297	5365

* = ENTRY ALTERED FROM SOURCE; #,@,>=RELATIVES NAMED IN SOURCE. EXPLANATIONS PAGE 11, FICHE U

A = ADULT CHRISTENING B = BIRTH C = CHRISTENING D = DEATH OR BURIAL F = BIRTH OR CHRISTENING OF FIRST KNOWN CHILD M = MARRIAGE N = CENSUS W = WILL ALL OTHERS = MISCELLANEOUS

Fig. 6.10. Extract from the IGI relating to Ireland. (Reprinted by permission. Copyright 1989 by the Corporation of the President of The Church of Jesus Christ of Latter-Day Saints.)

right-hand columns contain that information. The IGI is not a definitive record. There is a tendency for researchers to accept its information as indisputable, when in fact it contains errors; dates, spellings or locations may be incorrect, and the system used for indexing surnames is not one that most people are familiar with. Researchers are therefore advised to verify information with original sources wherever possible. The staff at Mormon family history centres will be pleased to advise.

Sources

The IGI will be found in Family History Centres of the Mormon church, addresses of which can be obtained from genealogical organisations or churches listed in the telephone directory under Church of Jesus Christ of Latter-Day Saints. It will also be found in the Public Record Office, London.

Computerisation

The IGI is currently being transferred onto computer and on completion is expected to contain around 200 million entries from around the world.

Deeds

Deeds are legally valid records of proof of sale of land and property and the means by which use or ownership was acquired. There are other kinds of deeds involving mortgages, marriage settlements, leases and wills, all of which are stored in the Registry of Deeds (RD) in Dublin (see Chapter 5). Deeds and their memorials (a synopsis of each deed) were sent to the RD where a summary of each memorial was transcribed into large volumes called Abstract Books and stored in the vaults of the building. The original deeds were returned to the relevant lawyer or agent. They were not retained in the RD.

The indexes

Indexes to this material were compiled in two parts, enabling researchers to locate and examine the relevant transcription of a memorial in the RD.

(a) Name Index: listing first named grantors (persons who sold or otherwise disposed of the property).

(b) Lands Index: arranged by townland within the relevant barony and county.

Computerisation

Since September 1990, the Names Index and Abstract Books have been replaced by computer.

Sources

Memorials and indexes can be examined in the RD for a small fee. Microfilmed copies of the indexes are available in the NLI and selected Mormon family history centres around the world.

Wills

From the early days of English administration, special courts of the Church of Ireland were responsible for 'probating' (validating) wills, and in the case of those who died 'intestate' (did not make a will), granting 'letters of administration' for the disposal of the property concerned. From 1858, the church ceased to administer this system. A Principal Registry was established in Dublin and District Registries were set up around Ireland. Those wills and administrations that had passed through the church courts were now transferred to the Public Record Office (later the National Archives) where they were transcribed into large volumes. Separate indexes to them were also compiled. Unfortunately, these wills, administrations and most of the transcripts were destroyed in 1922. The indexes, some of them damaged, survived.

Sources

Indexes to pre-1858 wills and administrations will be found in the NA as are calendars to post-1858 wills and administrations. Abstracts from post-1858 wills and some indexes from other sources had already been compiled prior to 1922. These are also in the NA. Other collections of wills and indexes will be found in the Registry of Deeds, National Library and Genealogical Office, Dublin. Will books from District Registries in Northern Ireland and a card index are in the PRONI. Due to their complexity, the subject of Deeds and Wills cannot be covered in depth here. They are nevertheless a rich source of information for family historians, naming in many instances spouses, children and relatives, together with details of land and property. Before commencing research into such material, readers are advised to acquire a basic knowledge of the subject. They are discussed in greater detail in *Irish Genealogy: A Record Finder*.

Records of the Royal Irish Constabulary (RIC)

The Irish Constabulary was established in 1836 by Sir Robert Peel to '. . . report and suppress disaffection of any kind . . .' Renamed the Royal Irish Constabulary, the force consisted of Irishmen until 1920 when Englishmen were encouraged to join owing to a lack of Irish recruits. In 1922, upon the establishment of an unarmed (Irish) force, the Garda Siochana, the RIC was disbanded. A separate force in the city of Dublin, the Dublin Metropolitan Police (DMP) amalgamated in 1925. Many RIC and DMP members re-enlisted in the new body whilst others resident in the north had the option of joining a new British force in Northern Ireland, the Royal Ulster Constabulary (RUC).

Sources

Copies of indexes listing individual officers and their service numbers are available in the National Archives, Dublin.

Also available are personnel registers containing details of each recruit and his spouse. These records are on microfilm. The original registers and indexes (HO 184) can be seen in the Public Record Office, London.

British Parliamentary Papers (BPPs)

For centuries, the affairs of Ireland have been recorded for the British parliament in London. From 1801, these were recorded in *British Parliamentary Papers* (BPPs) and included subjects as diverse as agriculture, civil registration, religion, coastguards, etc. Now comprising thousands of volumes, BPPs contain material of great historical and genealogical interest. The range of subjects covered are too numerous to list here but include such matters as vagrancy, landlordism, education, emigration, etc. in which all classes of people are identified. The Irish

University Press (IUP) has reprinted over 1,000 volumes of BPPs covering various subjects for the period 1801–1899.

The indexes

Over the years, various indexes have been compiled and some of these will be found alongside collections of Parliamentary Papers. A useful index published by Chadwyck-Healey contains detailed references to Irish matters. The IUP has also reprinted eight of the original general indexes for the period 1696–1907.

Sources

Collections of BPPs (not all of them complete) will be found in major repositories around the world, particularly those in former countries of the British Empire. Researchers overseas are encouraged to make local enquiries to ascertain availability.

In England, two major sources are the British Library (BL) and the Public Record Office (PRO) (see Chapter 5). The BL have more than 7,000 volumes of BPPs on open shelves which have been reproduced onto microfiche, enabling copies to be made without damaging the volumes. The volumes at the PRO can be photocopied using standard procedures. These will eventually be available only on microfiche.

Limitations

Only a limited amount of information can be obtained from official records and the quality of coverage will vary considerably. *Griffith's Valuation,* for example, whilst listing the names of occupiers and landowners, shows no other personal details. Similarly, *Tithe Applotment Books* show only occupiers' names. *British Parliamentary Papers* contain lists of names or personal details depending on the subject matter. To obtain further details, you should seek other information relating to the locality, individual or his occupation and once more interview your relatives, jogging their memories about what you have found.

Bibliography

Births and Deaths Registration (Ireland) Act 1863.

British Parliamentary Papers 1800–1900 (1000 volume series), Irish University Press (Irish Academic Press Ltd.), Dublin, 1977.

Cockton, Peter, *Subject Catalogue of the House of Commons Parliamentary Papers 1801–1900,* Chadwyck-Healy Ltd., Cambridge, 1988.

Connell, K.H., *The Population of Ireland 1750–1845,* Clarendon Press, Oxford, 1950.

ffolliott, Rosemary, Irish Census Returns and Census Substitutes, *Irish Genealogy: A Record Finder,* Heraldic Artists Ltd., Dublin, 1987.

ffolliott, Rosemary, The Registry of Deeds for Genealogical Purposes, *Irish Genealogy: A Record Finder,* Heraldic Artists Ltd., Dublin, 1987.

ffolliott, Rosemary and O'Byrne, Eileen, Wills and Administrations, *Irish Genealogy: A Record Finder,* Heraldic Artists Ltd., Dublin, 1987.

General Report of the Census of Ireland 1901, *British Parliamentary Papers,* HC 1902 CXXIX.

General Report of the Census of Ireland 1911, *British Parliamentary Papers,* HC 1912–13 CXVIII.

Grenham, John, *Tracing Your Irish Ancestors,* Gill and MacMillan, Dublin, 1992.

Guide to the Public Record Office of Northern Ireland, PRONI, Belfast, 1991.

Hayes, Richard J., *Manuscript Sources for the History of Irish Civilisation,* G.K. Hall, Boston, Massachusetts, 1965.

Hickey, D.J. and Doherty, J.E., *A Dictionary of Irish History 1800– 1980,* Gill and MacMillan, Dublin, reprinted 1989.

McCarthy, Tony (Ed.), *Irish Roots*, Vols. 1 and 2, Belgrave Publications, Cork.

McCarthy, Tony, *The Irish Roots Guide,* Lilliput Press, Dublin, 1991.

McDowell, R.B., *The Irish Administration 1801–1914,* Routledge and Keegan Paul, 1964.

Marriages (Ireland) Act 1844.

Nolan, William, *Tracing the Past: Sources for Local Studies in the Republic of Ireland,* Geography Publications, Dublin, 1982.

Registration of Marriages (Ireland) Act 1863.

Return of Owners of Land of One Acre and Upwards in Counties, Cities and Towns in Ireland, *British Parliamentary Papers,* HC 1876 LXXX.

Return of Owners of Land of One Acre and Upwards in Counties, Cities and Towns in Ireland, Alexander Thom, Dublin, 1876; reprinted 1988 by Genealogical Publishing Co. Inc., Baltimore, Massachusetts.

Sources for Family History and Genealogy, National Archives, Dublin (1988)

Chapter 7

WHERE DO YOU GO FROM HERE?

The possibilities

For many descendants, Irish research is an enigma, and the barriers of distance, time and cost effectively prevent travel to Ireland, so what can be done in this situation? The fact that you have read this far indicates your determination to do something, and the previous chapters will have shown the possibilities of postal research, but can any more be done without travelling to Ireland?

Research in the host country

The answer is yes, and provided the rules in Chapters 1 and 2 were followed, you will have at least some information concerning your ancestors' settlement. A knowledge of genealogical records in the host country (where your ancestors settled) is therefore important, and you can obtain literature on the subject from your local library or bookshop (see Chapters 3 and 4). The recording of information about individuals and their settlement in the host country is one of the functions of genealogical organisations worldwide. Some of this information is published in their journals.

Advertisements

It is not unusual to place advertisements in newspapers requesting help for information about ancestors. This may be done in the last known country of residence or in Ireland itself. Replies may be elicited from descendants or persons acquainted with the family. Local Irish newspapers are increasingly used by family historians and genealogists seeking information about ancestors. In Co. Clare, for example, the *Clare Champion* frequently publishes genealogical requests in their 'letters' column. One correspondent in Australia even included an e-mail address for replies to be sent via the Internet (see also The Internet).

Membership of family history societies can help in this respect through their journals many of which contain a section for members' interests. For example, in an Australian journal, *The Genealogist,* one member required information about John Barford, an Irish convict who "... came to trial in Dublin County in 1806, age 35. Sentenced to life ... arrived in New South Wales in 1809 ... In 1811, he married Elizabeth Church, (also) an Irish convict who ... (had been) ... sentenced to 7 years ... John was pardoned in 1813 bringing two persons to conviction for illegal distillation ..."

Requests for information about ancestors and their occupations may also appear in specialist publications. John R. Carrey writing in *Sea Breezes,* a magazine about ships and the sea asked "Can any reader help me to trace information on the ships owned by my Northern Irish family during the last century, and particularly the 166-ton brigantine *Carrickfergus,* named after the Ulster town where she was built in 1845? (sic). My great-great-grandfather, Capt. John Carrey, was master and owner on her final voyage from Antwerp to Buenos Aires when she was 'lost' off the Spanish coast on June 6, 1860. All hands were saved ...

See also **Family history societies,** below.

Reference libraries

Reference libraries around the world should not be ignored. From these, readers can obtain books on many related subjects, i.e. famine, emigration, the Irish in Britain, America, etc., such material providing valuable background information for those researching ancestry.

Family history societies

Membership of genealogical or family history organisations is a positive step towards your goal, for you will meet people with active interests in the field of genealogical research. You will also discover information about Irish research.

Australia

For example, in Australia, a country that swarmed with immigrants from 1787, a number of research organisations cater for members' specific interests. The Genealogical Society of Victoria contains an Irish Ancestry Group whose members are involved in Irish research and publish a newsletter, the *Blarney*. Elsewhere in Australia, the Western Australian Genealogical Society have published an *Irish Interests Directory.*

Canada

Australian societies are not unique in this respect. The Ottawa branch of the Ontario Genealogical Society boasts an Irish Research group which produced a guide book *Basic Irish Genealogical Sources: Description and Evaluation* relating to Irish research in Ontario. There is also news that Montreal is setting up an Irish heritage centre.

United States of America

In the USA, the Chicago Genealogical Society has formed an Irish Interest Group and the Minnesota Genealogical Society also contains an Irish section.

New Zealand

The New Zealand Society of Genealogists has an Irish Interest Group. In 1991, details of its material and future events created excitement:

"The Irish Special Interest Group has purchased the latest Deputy Keepers Reports of Northern Ireland, 1966–1986 . . . We have compiled six extra pages with . . . film numbers of some of the records to order at the LDS Family History Libraries including the records of . . . Irish County Militia Units, Royal Irish Constabulary and Customs and Excise . . . The Irish Group Melbourne has a two day weekend in May. The Irish Group will bring research to the Hastings conference in May and Joe Cassin will bring his Irish library."

England

Because of the number of members who are Irish descendants (see Chapter 3), the Manchester and Lancashire Family History Society in England has formed an Irish Ancestry Group and includes in its journal a section devoted to news about Irish research. The group is considering a project to extract and record all Irish born persons in the 1861 Manchester census. It also possesses on microfiche *Griffith's Valuation,* thereby enabling members to examine this material without having to visit Ireland.

Also in England, the foremost organisation concerned with Irish research is the Irish Genealogical Research Society (IGRS). Established in London in 1936, it has a branch in Ireland and a membership of almost 1,000, many of whom reside overseas. 'Institutional' membership includes organisations and archives around the world connected in some way with Irish research. A list of members will be found in its journal *The Irish Genealogist.*

The IGRS welcomes visitors to its premises in London where there is a remarkable collection of Irish material dating from the 17th century. More recent material includes the 19th century *Griffith's Valuation* on microfiche (Chapter 6) and the *Townland Index* of 1901 (Chapter 1). The society is so popular, that an American group includes it in an annual tour (see Appendix B).

Ireland

Genealogical organisations in Ireland also include overseas membership. Prominent among these are the Irish Family History Society, Co. Kildare, the North of Ireland Family History Society and Ulster-Scot Historical Foundation, Belfast. Other societies are being formed around the country and currently attract enquiries from around the world.

The English connection

If enquiries reveal that your ancestors emigrated via England (Chapter 3), you will need to find out more information, perhaps contacting English sources and conducting further research by mail. But how do you obtain information about the Irish in Britain if you reside overseas? An obvious method is to obtain books from libraries and bookshops; another is this. Most genealogical organisations publish journals, some of which include articles of specific/local interest to researchers in other countries. *The Family History News and Digest* (FHN&D), published by the Federation of Family History Societies (FFHS), contains references to such items gleaned from journals of organisations around the world. Examples include:

Some English Poor Law Records and their Usefulness to the Family Historian, by Barbara Robinson, in *New Zealand Genealogist,* Vol. 19, No. 181, New Zealand Society of Genealogists, Jan/Feb 1988 (FHN&D, Vol. 7, No. 2).

Sources for Lancashire, by R.J.Bond, in *Genealogist's Magazine,* Vol. 23, Nos. 2 and 3, Society of Genealogists, London, Jun/Sept 1989 (FHN&D, Vol. 7, No. 3).

1843 Immigrant's Diary, by Thomas Eadie, in *Family Footsteps,* Vol. 5, No. 2, Kamloops FHS, Canada, Oct 1989. Tells of crossing the Atlantic (FHN&D, Vol. 7, No. 3).

Tracing Emigrant Ancestors to North America, by N. Currer-Briggs, in *Journal of the Cambridgeshire Family History Society,* Vol. 8, No. 8, Nov 1992. Helpful advice for research in the period covering 17th–19th century (FHN&D, Vol. 9, No. 1)

Items more directly concerned with Irish research include:

The Irish Connection, by Godfrey Duffy, in *Journal of The Northumberland and Durham FHS,* Vol. 15, No. 2, Summer 1990. How one member solved his Irish problems (FHN&D, Vol. 8, No. 1).

Sources for Study of Emigration from Ulster to New Zealand 1840–1940, by Trevor Parkhill, in *GRINZ Yearbook,* Genealogical Research Institute of New Zealand, 1988. Emigration records at PRONI, Belfast, including collections of letters from Ulster men and women who settled in many parts of the world in the 19th century (FHN&D, Vol. 7, No. 1).

Irish Transportation Records. How to use them, by Dawn Montgomery, in *Queensland Family Historian,* Vol. 9, No. 6, Queensland FHS, Australia, Dec 1988 (FHN&D, Vol. 7, No. 2).

Back-copies of journals can be obtained from the relevant society. Their addresses will be found in the *Family History News and Digest.*

Members' interests

Many of the journals contain sections devoted to members' interests where members advertise their requirements to a wider audience. An existing scheme, whereby societies exchange their journals with those of others, ensures that such interests are given worldwide coverage. An example is supplied by the author who advertised in an English journal his interest concerning a 19th century Irish family. He subsequently received a letter from descendants in New Zealand who had seen the exchange journal. *Family History News and Digest* can be obtained from affiliated organisations or direct from the FFHS.

Other publications

Irish Roots magazine

In the Spring of 1992, The magazine *Irish Roots* made its appearance. Aimed at Irish descendants worldwide, it contained items connected with Irish research and culture. *Irish Roots* now boasts readers around the world. (See Appendix B.)

Family Tree Magazine

Of general interest, the *Family Tree Magazine* is well established worldwide. Aimed at readers of British descent, its articles cover a range of subjects and countries, including Ireland. A separate index is published periodically. (See Appendix B.)

Familia

Aimed at Irish descendants worldwide, *Familia* contains a variety of articles about Irish genealogy many of them with an Ulster flavour. (See Appendix B.)

Visiting Ireland

When planning to visit Ireland for research purposes, the keyword is caution. You do not want to arrive and find archives closed due to renovation, staff sickness or national holidays. One researcher, intent on spending all his time in a local history centre, arrived to discover it was closed for two weeks because the archivist was on holiday. It is good practice to contact archives before your visit to ascertain opening times and any other circumstances affecting the availability of records. With this information, you can then compile a 'visiting plan'.

Doing your homework

Chapter 1 commented on the fact that many family historians travel thousands of miles to Ireland with little idea of how to begin their research. Whilst holidaying in Ireland, Frances Brown observed this happening. Writing in *The Genealogist* she said:

> After leaving Limerick, I visited a number of genealogical repositories in Dublin. I heard Australians making enquiries about their family history. They hadn't done enough research back in Australia and had lots of 'abouts' and 'I thinks'. . . information could have been found before making the trip . . . (That) information might be essential to success in Ireland. The reality comes from being prepared, knowing what information is essential and taking it with you. It also means knowing what records exist in Ireland and where to find them.

Those were words of wisdom. Frances should know. She is currently the Genealogy and Local History Librarian at the State Library of Victoria, Australia. The Association of County Archivists in England is also noted for wisdom. Their Guide *You and Your Record Office* states:

> You will find a visit to a record office much more rewarding if you do your homework beforehand and arrive well prepared. You should be quite clear about what you want to find out . . . This means collecting all the known facts about your family first and deciding what you hope to find out on your visit. If you are a beginner your first step, before a visit, should be to read a book . . .

Warning

You are the only person interested in your family history. When visiting archives, curb the impulse to chatter about your ancestry. Not only does it disrupt other people's study, it will identify you as a 'bore' and a person to be avoided at all costs, thus ruining any chance you may have had of obtaining extra help. Sadly, it is also a fact that in the past valuable material has been mistreated by self-professed ancestor hunters displaying a lack of respect for staff, records and other researchers.

Local contacts

You will already have made, through letters of enquiry (Chapter 2), cordial relationships with one or two local people who may be willing to assist you during your visit. A short letter informing them of your intentions and requesting their help is a reasonable method of approach. The Irish people are warm and generous and respond to a reasonable approach. A cup of tea made from the kettle boiling permanently on the range is usually a sign that things are going well. Susan Allaby of Aylesbury, Buckinghamshire was overcome by her reception:

> "On two visits to Ireland, we received wonderful hospitality wherever we went. I cannot stress how helpful and trusting we found all the people we met . . . from the owners of my former ancestral homes, to the man working in New Ross churchyard, time was the most valuable thing given to us . . ."

Libraries in Ireland

City and county libraries in Ireland are useful sources for genealogical research and hold a variety of material relating to particular areas and inhabitants. Bob Philpott of Kenilworth, Warwickshire, was impressed by their staff:

> "In Cork, where I spent several days in the library, I had kind assistance from two of the archivists . . ."

Inge Veecock of Ealing, London, found staff very helpful:

> ". . . the Waterford Municipal Library gave me good advice and searched many sources for me."

And E.W. Doherty of Alton, Hampshire received a surprise:

> "The Waterford City library . . . are very obliging, sending me a book *Memories of Waterford* gratis, and a summary of their holdings. The county library at Lismore have sent me a guide to Co. Waterford."

Some libraries have published lists of their holdings, and one such publication, *Sligo: Sources of Local History, A Catalogue of the Local History Collection, with an Introduction and Guide to Sources,* compiled by the County Librarian of Sligo, John C. McTernan, deserves particular mention.

Extracts from McTernan's introduction explain the relationship between local history and genealogical research, and the usefulness of such material:

"In the recent past we have witnessed an ever increasing interest in local history. More than ever before people are anxious to know something about their roots, who they are and where they came from, and this, in turn, has given rise to an increasing interest in a wide range of Local Studies."

"Family history and the tracing of ancestors is an engrossing occupation for many, and the local collection will frequently be called upon to assist enquirers, both in person and by letter, often from the United States or far-off Australia."

But readers would do well to heed his cautionary note which can be taken as applicable to all libraries and archives:

"Although it is not the function of the library to undertake research work on behalf of individuals, if staffing permits, a limited amount of assistance is usually provided. In cases where more detailed examination of records is called for, the enquirer is referred to a professional researcher."

His catalogue lays out with exceptional clarity, over 2,500 items grouped under 34 different subject headings and is currently undergoing revision. It is, at the very least, an example of how archivists can help family and local historians.

Other sources in Ireland

As already stated, county and city libraries can be of great help to those researching ancestry but there are other sources seldom used by family historians. Some counties have local history centres containing material of an historical or genealogical nature. A good example is the Clare County Library Local Studies Centre in Ennis. Contained in its collection is *Griffith's Valuation, Tithe Applotment Books,* maps of the Ordnance Survey and microfilmed 18th and 19th century estate records listing tenants on local estates. (See Chapter 6.) Other sources around Ireland consist of local exhibitions showing the growth of villages and displaying documents and photographs of interest to those with roots in the area. An exhibition in Co. Clare, Kilrush in Landlord Times, is particularly useful for those researching estate papers and Emigrants, Two Centuries of Emigration is the theme for another exhibition in the Ulster American Folk Park, Omagh, Co. Tyrone. Kerry Bog Village in Glenbeigh, Co. Kerry is an unusual development recreating early 19th century village life and Bunratty Folk Park in Co. Clare has constructed old shops and cottages with real turf fires. Researchers should enquire as to the location of such exhibitions, bearing in mind that some may be of short duration whilst others are permanent.

Walking

Whilst on the subject of localities, descendants visiting Ireland should not miss the opportunity of walking through the countryside where they may still see remnants of ancestral homes which are fast disappearing. Tourist offices around Ireland are able to

275   BALL-WRIGHT, W.   & PHIBBS, O.

Pedigree of the Phibbs Family since their settlement
in Ireland.
Sligo, 1890.   36p.

276   BARTLETT, T.

The O'Haras of Annaghmore, c. 1600 - 1800: Survival
and revival.
18p.
[In "Jr. of Econ. & Soc. Hist. Society of Ireland",
  Vol. 9, 1982].   L.H./13

277   BURKE, B.

Landed gentry of County Sligo.
54p.
[Extracts from Burke's "Lande d Gentry of Ireland" &
  "Irish Family Records". 1904 - 1976].

278   BYRNE, C.

Hillas of County Sligo.
4p.
[In "Irish Ancestor", 4 (i), 1972].

279   CLESHAM, B.

Introduction and descriptive list of the Family
Papers of the Ormsbys of Ballinamore and Cummin,
together with copies of extracts.
28p.   [Typescript].

280   CROFTON, H.T.

The Croftons of Longford House and Templehouse.
70p.   ports.
[In "Crofton Memoirs", York, 1911].

281   DALTON, J.

Memoir of the Family of King.
28p.
[In Dalton's "Annals of Boyle", Vol. 1,
  Dublin, 1845].

Fig. 7.1. Extract from McTernan's *Sligo. Sources of Local History.*

recommend routes and areas to visit but visitors to North Clare have been given a bonus. They can now obtain the walking guide *North Clare Wonderland* showing in map form a series of walks around an area of natural beauty called 'The Burren'. Primarily famous for its limestone pavements, rare flora and archaeology, visitors with varying interests will find much to interest them:

... on your right is Poll Mhor a 10 hectare valley surrounded by cliffs and forts. Here, badgers, foxes, hares and rabbits share the peacefulness of nature ... a stretch of bogland, fenced fields and cattle grazing peacefully ... a round castle built by the O'Connors, and held by the O'Briens and Mac Clancys. It fell into ruin and was restored in the 70s by an American millionaire, John O'Gorman ... at your feet are rafts of Burren flora, steel blue gentians, dazzling purple cranesbill, pink orchids ... further on your right is Poulnabrone Domen, world famous, excavated and repaired in 1987. The remains of 16 adults and 6 children were interred there ... Flint stone tools and a pendant were also buried ...

Visitors will be pleased to note that Clare Heritage and Genealogical Centre is situated on the edge of the Burren in the town of Corofin. (See Appendix B.)

Clan rallies

Clan rallies, for those who feel they are associated with particular surnames, are now held regularly in Ireland. Considered by some to be more appropriate in Scotland than Ireland, their activities are not necessarily part of serious genealogical research. However, encouraged by the Irish Tourist Board and other bodies, they have become popular with tourists and Irish descendants abroad. Further information about Clan events can be obtained from the Clans of Ireland Office in Dublin. (See Appendix B.)

Research centres

Most counties in Ireland now have research or heritage centres engaged in transcribing and indexing local records from which information is available on payment of a fee. A list of centres will be found in Appendix A. Some centres advertise on the internet and give details of their services. (See also The Internet.) It is thought by some that the presence of research centres implies that personal research is a thing of the past. That is not so. Research can still be conducted as before and enquiries made by following the procedures described in this book.

The Internet

The Internet is a global network of computers, commercial and private, all linked together. Originally established by academic and research communities as a means of sharing information, the system is now estimated to link over 50 million computers around the world. Anyone with a computer can obtain information about any subject including genealogy. Family history societies and genealogical organisations find this an efficient method of advertising and publishing genealogical information.

There is also much about Irish research not only from Irish-related organisations but also from individuals seeking ancestors or sharing information about their own research. Individuals can also communicate with others of similar interests around the world via e-mail (electronic mail).

Conferences and other events

Today, in countries that were subject to Irish emigration, genealogical institutions regularly organise conferences that include an Irish flavour. During 1988, one such event (Seminar '88) was held at Ottawa University, Canada, in which a major theme was The Irish Connection. In November of the same year, the Australian Genealogical Society of Victoria organised an Irish Origins conference. The following year in Sydney, the Society of Australian Genealogists conducted an Irish seminar, and in Ireland, the Second International Irish Origins Conference was held in Kilkenny Castle.

Probably the largest function of its kind was the First Irish Genealogical Congress held at Trinity College, Dublin, in September 1991, and attended by visitors from around the world. Sponsored by genealogical and historical societies, it provided 54 lectures, an exhibition, bookstalls, workshops, research advisory service, and a Question and Answer session. A sight-seeing programme was even arranged for husbands and wives not interested in their spouses' hobby. Following on from this, the Genealogical Office published a 215 page book *Aspects of Irish Genealogy* containing a selection of lectures given by speakers at the conference. This book can be obtained from the Genealogical Office in Dublin. The event was repeated in 1994 and 1997 in Dublin and Maynooth respectively.

In 1993, the Ulster Historical Foundation hosted a two-part conference, the first part held in Jordanstown and the second in Dublin.

Things were also happening elsewhere. Since 1993 family history fairs organised by the Society of Genealogists were held in London. Ireland was represented with stands manned by the Ulster Historical Foundation, Irish Family History Society, Flyleaf Press, *Irish Roots Magazine* and Irish Genealogical Research Society. There is now much to interest Irish descendants and conferences/seminars with an Irish flavour have become common place around the world. Details of such events will be found in genealogical publications.

Reports about past events can be equally interesting and researchers can pick up useful information from these. In British Columbia, for example, a seminar was organised by the Kamloops Family History Society in 1994 at which several well-known persons in British and Canadian genealogy gave presentations. A report in *The British Columbia Genealogist* summarised each talk. Irish descendants listening to Terence Punch were surprised to learn that relatives and neighbours of Irish emigrants often followed them, settling in the same area. Some emigrants did not arrive from Ireland but were themselves descendants of Irish who had previously settled in other countries and now had non-Irish surnames. Useful information for descendants overseas.

Tour companies organise trips to Irish castles and other buildings associated with Irish surnames and visitors flock to research/heritage centres looking for information about their ancestors. Family history organisations facilitate worldwide contact with those of similar interests and international publications such as the *Family Tree Magazine, Irish Roots* and *Familia* help descendants to keep in touch with the world of ancestral research. One of the organisers of the First Irish Genealogical Congress, Paul Gorry, writing in the *Family Tree Magazine,* sees a purpose in meetings and conferences:

"... there is much more to them than the lectures that form their essential base. Spending a few days at such a gathering, you cannot help bumping into ancestor-addicts at breakfast, lunch and dinner . . . you will emerge from the experience with all sorts of contacts and tips. Apart from anything else, you will have fun."

As the *Ancestor* puts it, such conferences:

". . . create deeper interest in Ireland itself . . . they encourage Irish researchers; geographers; family historians; genealogists; archaeologists; archivists; and local history societies to bring together all the varied information on localities and persons."

They also demonstrate that something is being done about the problems of Irish research.

Bibliography

Ancestor, Vol. 19, Nos. 3, 4, 7, Genealogical Society of Victoria, Australia, 1989.

Aspects of Irish Genealogy: Proceedings of the 1st Irish Genealogical Congress, 1st Irish Genealogical Congress Committee, Dublin.

Bagley, Gary Allen et al., *Basic Irish Genealogical Sources: Description and Evaluation,* Ontario Genealogical Society, Ottawa, 1993.

Brown, Frances, Notes From the State Library of Victoria, *The Genealogist,* Vol. VII, No. 4, Australian Institute of Genealogical Studies, Victoria, 1992.

Families, Vol. 32, No. 4, Ontario Genealogical Society, Toronto, Ontario, 1993.

Family History News and Digest, Vols. 7–9, Federation of Family History Societies, Birmingham.

Internetting, Kelsey Publishing Ltd., Surrey, 1997.

The Genealogist, Vol. VII, No. 9, Australian Institute of Genealogical Studies, Victoria, 1994.

Gorry, Paul, Irish Genealogical Congress, *Family Tree Magazine,* Vol. 7, No. 2, 1990.

McTernan, John C., *Sligo: Sources of Local History,* Sligo County Library, 1988.

The Manchester Genealogist, Vol. 25, No. 3, Manchester and Lancashire Family History Society, 1989.

The Manchester Genealogist, Vol. 30, No. 1, Manchester and Lancashire Family History Society, 1989.

Newsleaf, Vol. 18, No. 1, Ontario Genealogical Society Supplement, 1988.

The New Zealand Genealogist, Vol. 22, No. 208, New Zealand Society of Genealogists, Auckland, 1991.

The New Zealand Genealogist, Vol. 24, No. 221, New Zealand Society of Genealogists, Auckland, 1993.

North Clare Wonderland: Walking Guide, Leader Tourism Promotions, Lisdoonvarna.

Programme: 1st Irish Genealogical Congress 1991, Congress Office, Dublin, 1991.

Sea Breezes, Vol. 68, No. 581, Kinglish Ltd., Douglas, Isle of Man, 1994.

Sharon, Margaret M., *Kamloops Family History Society Seminar,* The British Columbia Genealist, Vol. 22, No. 2, British Columbia Genealogical Society, Canada, 1993.

You and Your Record Office: A Code of Practice for Family Historians, Association of County Archivists in conjunction with the Federation of Family History Societies, 2nd edn., 1990.

Western Ancestor, Vol. 4, No. 12, Western Australian Genealogical Society, 1990.

Appendix A

HERITAGE AND RESEARCH CENTRES
IN IRELAND

To alleviate growing unemployment in Ireland during the late 1970s, work-training schemes were set up involving 'projects of archaeological or historical merit'. Because parish registers were the sole historical records in many areas, related indexing projects were established in centres around the country. The scheme, currently receiving international funding, intends making the results available for a fee. The project is not confined to parish records, and other material has been collected relating to specific areas. Much of this is being computerised. Most counties have centres engaged in this work and some have already completed the task. Heritage centres, as they have become known, welcome enquiries from around the world and will forward details of their services upon receipt of an SAE/SASE or IRC.

The following is a list of centres throughout Ireland which was correct at the time of writing. All efforts have been made to ensure accuracy but changes will occur. Readers are advised to establish contact prior to making further arrangements.

Co. Antrim
Name:The Ulster Historical Foundation
Address:Balmoral Buildings, 12 College Square East, Belfast BT1 6DD

Co. Armagh
Name: Armagh Ancestry
Address: 42 English Street, Armagh City BT60 7BA, Co. Armagh

Co. Carlow
Name: Carlow County Family Heritage Research Ltd.
Address: c/o Old CBS, College Street, Carlow Town, Co. Carlow
(No research service yet.)

Co. Cavan
Name: Co. Cavan Genealogical Research Centre
Address: Cana House, Farnham Street, Cavan Town, Co. Cavan

Co. Clare
Name: Clare Heritage and Genealogical Centre
Address: Church Street, Corofin, Co. Clare

Co. Cork

Cork North
Name: Mallow Heritage Centre
Address: 27–28 Bank Place, Mallow, Co. Cork
Cork City
Name: Cork Ancestry
Address: c/o Cork County Library, Farranlea Road, Cork City, Co. Cork
(Full service not yet offered.)

Co. Derry

See Co. Londonderry.

Co. Donegal

Name: Donegal Ancestry
Address: Old Meeting House, Back Lane, Ramelton, Co. Donegal

Co. Down

No research centre. Enquiries handled by the Ulster Historical Foundation. See Co. Antrim.

Co. Dublin

Dublin South
Name: Dun Laoghaire Heritage Society
Address: Moran Park House, Dun Laoghaire, Co. Dublin
Dublin North
Name: Fingal Heritage Group
Address: Carnegie Library, North Street, Swords, Co. Dublin

Co. Fermanagh

No research centre. Enquiries handled by Heritage World. See Co. Tyrone.

Co. Galway

Galway West
Name: Galway Family History Society West Ltd.
Address: Unit 3, Venture Centre, Liosbaun Estate, Tuam Road, Co. Galway
Galway East
Name: East Galway Family History Society
Address: Woodford Heritage Centre, Woodford, Co. Galway

Co. Kerry

Name: Killarney Genealogical Centre
Address: Cathedral Walk, Killarney, Co. Kerry

Co. Kildare

Name: Co. Kildare Heritage and Genealogy Company
Address: c/o Kildare County Library, Newbridge, Co. Kildare

Co. Kilkenny

Name: Kilkenny Ancestry
Address: Rothe House, Parliament Street, Kilkenny City, Co. Kilkenny

King's County

See Co. Offaly

Co. Laois or Leix (formerly Queen's County)

No research centre. Enquiries handled by Co. Offaly (q.v.)

Co. Leitrim

Name: Leitrim Genealogy Centre
Address: County Library, Ballinamore,Co. Leitrim

Co. Limerick

Name: Limerick Regional Archives
Address: The Granary, Michael Street, Limerick City, Co. Limerick

Co. Londonderry

Name: Genealogy Centre
Address: 4–22, Butcher Street, Londonderry City BT48 6HL, Co. Londonderry

Co. Longford

Name: Longford Roots
Address: 1, Church Street, Longford Town, Co. Longford

Co. Louth

No research centre. Enquiries handled by Co. Meath (q.v.)

Co. Mayo

Mayo North
Name: Family Heritage Centre Ltd.
Address: Enniscoe, Castle Hill, Co. Mayo
Mayo South
Name: South Mayo Family Research Centre
Address: Town Hall, Ballinrobe, Co. Mayo

Co. Meath

Name: Meath Heritage and Genealogy Centre
Address: Mill Street, Trim, Co. Meath

Co. Monaghan

Name: Monaghan Ancestry
Address: 6, Tully, Monaghan Town, Co. Monaghan

Co. Offaly (formerly Kings County)

Name: Family History Research
Address: Bury Quay, Tullamore, Co. Offaly

Queen's County
See Co. Laois

Roscommon
Name: Co. Roscommon Heritage and Genealogy Centre
Address: Church Street, Strokestown, Co. Roscommon

Co. Sligo
Name: Co. Sligo Heritage and Genealogical Centre
Address: Aras Reddan, Temple Street, Sligo Town, Co. Sligo

Co. Tipperary

Tipperary North
Name: Tipperary North Family History Research Centre
Address: The Gatehouse, Kickham Street, Nenagh, Co. Tipperary

Tipperary South
Name: Bru Boru Heritage Centre
Address: Cashel, Co. Tipperary

Tipperary Town
Name: Tipperary Heritage Unit
Address: The Bridewell, St. Michael's Street, Tipperary Town, Co. Tipperary

Co. Tyrone
Name: Heritage World
Address: 26, Market Square, Dungannon, Co. Tyrone, BT70 1AB

Co. Waterford
Name: Waterford Heritage Genealogical Service
Address: St. Patrick's Church, Jenkin's Lane, Waterford City, Co. Waterford

Co. Westmeath
Name: Dun Na Si Heritage Centre
Address: Moate, Co. Westmeath

Co. Wexford
Name: Tagoat Community Development
Address: Tagoat, Rosslare, Co. Wexford

Co. Wicklow
Name: Wicklow Heritage Centre
Address: The Court House, Wicklow Town, Co. Wicklow

USEFUL ADDRESSES

The following is a selection of repositories and organisations holding Irish or Irish-related material, or providing services in connection with Irish research. Readers are advised to contact sources to ascertain services offered, or the extent and availability of material relative to their enquiries.

BRITAIN

Archives

British Library (BL):
 (a) The British Museum, Great Russell Street, London WC1B 3DG
 (b) 96, Euston Street, London NW1 2DB
 Material is currently being transferred from (a) to (b). Both locations are open. Enquirers should contact the BL to ascertain the location of material relevant to their research.

British Library Newspaper Library, Colindale Avenue, Colindale, London NW7 5HE

Central Reference Library, William Brown Street, Liverpool L3 8EW

Merseyside Maritime Museum, Albert Dock, Liverpool L3 4AA

Public Record Office (PRO), Ruskin Avenue, Kew, Richmond, Surrey TW9 4DU

National Library of Wales, Aberystwyth, Dyfed SY23 3BU

National Library of Scotland, George IV Bridge, Edinburgh EH1 1EW

Scottish Record Office (SRO):
 (a) Old Register House, Princes Street, Edinburgh, EH1 3YY
 (b) West Register House, Charlotte Square, Edinburgh
 (c) New Register House, Princes Street, Edinburgh, EH1 3YT

Associations

Association of Genealogists and Record Agents (AGRA), 29, Badgers Close, Horsham, West Sussex RH12 5RU
 Some members live in Ireland and specialise in Irish research.

Association of Scottish Genealogists and Record Agents (ASGRA), P.O. Box 174, Edinburgh EH3 5QZ

British Records Association, 18, Padbury Court, London E2 7EH

Federation of Family History Societies (FFHS), c/o The Benson Room, Birmingham and Midland Institute, Margaret Street, Birmingham B3 3BS

Irish Genealogical Research Society (IGRS), c/o The Irish Club, 82, Eaton Square, London SW1W 9AJ
 Entrance in Lyall Street.

Society of Genealogists (SOG), 14, Charterhouse Buildings, Goswell Road, London EC1M 7BA

Civil registration

Family Records Centre, 1, Myddelton Street, Islington, London EC1R 1UW

General Register Office for Scotland, New Register House, Princes Street, Edinburgh EH1 3YT

Miscellaneous

Irish Tourist Board, New Bond Street, London

Family Tree Magazine, 61, Great Whyte, Ramsey, Huntingdon, Cambridgeshire, PE17 1HL

Kinglish Ltd., Douglas, Isle of Man

IRELAND

Archives

Genealogical Office (GO), 2, Kildare Street, Dublin 2

Military Archives, Cathal Brugha Barracks, Rathmines, Dublin 6
   Advance notice required.

National Archives (NA):

   (a) Bishops Street, Dublin 8
   Headquarters of the National Archives. Contains material transferred from the Four Courts, Office of Public Works and State Paper Office

   (b) Four Courts, Dublin 7
   Now closed. Formerly the Public Record Office, all records have been transferred to Bishops Street.

   (c) Office of Public Works, Dublin 7.
   Now closed. All records have been transferred to Bishops Street.

   (d) State Paper Office, Dublin Castle
   Now closed. All records have been transferred to Bishops Street.

National Library of Ireland (NLI), Kildare Street, Dublin 2

Public Record Office of Northern Ireland (PRONI), 66, Balmoral Avenue, Belfast BT9 6NY

Registry of Deeds (RD), Henrietta Street, Dublin 1

Representative Church Body Library (RCBL), Braemor Park, Rathgar, Dublin 14

Valuation Office, 6, Ely Place, Dublin 2

Associations

Association of Professional Genealogists in Ireland (APGI), The Genealogical Office, 2, Kildare Street, Dublin 2

Association of Ulster Genealogists and Record Agents (AUGRA), Glen Cottage, Glenmachan Road, Belfast BT4 2NP

Irish Family History Society, P.O. Box 36, Naas, Co. Kildare

Irish Genealogical Association, 164 Kingsway, Dunmurry, Belfast, Northern Ireland BT17 9AD

Irish Genealogical Research Society, 6, Eaton Brae, Orwell Road, Dublin 14

North of Ireland Family History Society, Department of Education, Queen's University, 69 University Street, Belfast BT7 1HL

Presbyterian Historical Society of Ireland, Church House, Fisherwick Place, Belfast BT1 6DW
Now closed. Records deposited at the Belfast Central Library, Royal Avenue, Belfast BT1 1EA.

Religious Society of Friends in Ireland:

(a) Swanbrook House, Morehampton Road, Dublin 4

(b) Meeting House, Railway Street, Lisburn, Co. Antrim
Postal enquiries only.

Ulster Historical Foundation, 12 College Square East, Belfast, BT1 6DD

Ulster-Scot Historical Foundation, 66 Balmoral Avenue, Belfast, Northern Ireland BT9 6NY

Civil registration

The General Register Office (GRO), 8–11 Lombard Street East, Dublin 2

The General Register Office of Northern Ireland (GRONI), Oxford House, 49–55 Chichester Street, Belfast BT1 4HL

Miscellaneous

Clans of Ireland Office, 2 Kildare Street, Dublin 2

Irish Genealogical Congress Committee, Genealogical Office, 2 Kildare Street, Dublin 2

Irish Microforms Ltd., 10 Cornelscourt Hill, Foxrock, Dublin 18

Irish Roots Magazine, Belgrave Publications, Belgrave Avenue, Cork City

Irish Academic Press, Kill Lane, Blackrock, Co. Dublin

Irish University Press, now Irish Academic Press (q.v.)

Leader Tourism Promotions, Head Office, Lisdoonvarna, Co. Clare

United States of America

Archives

Boston Public Library, 666 Boyleston Street, Boston, Massachusetts, MA 62117

Library of Congress, Independence Avenue S.E., Washington DC 20540

National Archives, Pennsylvania Avenue, Washington DC 20408

New York State Archives, Cultural Education Centre, Empire State Plaza, Albany, NY 12230

New York Public Library, Fifth Avenue at 42nd Street, NY 10018

Associations

Association of Professional Genealogists (APG), P.O. Box 1161, Salt Lake City, UT 84147

Board of Certification of Genealogists, 1307 New Hampshire Avenue, NW Washington DC 20036

Chicago Irish Ancestry, c/o The Newberry Library, 60 West Walton, Chicago IL 60610

Genealogical Library, 35 North West Temple, Salt Lake City, UT 84150

Federation of Genealogical Societies, 2324 East Nottingham, Springfield, MO 65804–7821

International Society for British Genealogy and Family History, (ISBGFH), P.O. Box 20425, Cleveland, OH 44120–0425

The Irish Ancestral Research Association (TIARA), P.O. Box 616, Sudbury, MA 01776

Irish Genealogical Society, c/o Minnesota Genealogical Society, P.O. Box 16069, St. Paul, MN 55116

Irish Interest Group, Chicago Genealogical Society, P.O. Box 1160, Chicago, IL 60690

Civil registration (Vital Records)

Held by the relevant archives in each State.

Miscellaneous

The Genealogical Publishing Co. Inc., 1001 N. Calvert Street, Baltimore, MA 21202

The Irish Tourist Board Offices, 757 Third Avenue, NY 10017

Canada

Archives

National Archives of Canada, 395 Wellington Street, Ottawa K1A ON3

Associations

The British Columbia Genealogical Society, P.O. Box 88054, Richmond BC V6X 3T6

Canadian Federation of Genealogical and Family History Societies, 40 Celtic Bay, Winnipeg, Manitoba R3T 2W9

Ontario Genealogical Society, 40 Orchard View Blvd., Suite 251, Toronto, Ontario

Civil registration (vital records)

Held by the relevant archives in each Province.

Australia

Archives

Heraldry and Genealogy Society of Canberra, GPO Box 585, Canberra, ACT 2601

National Library of Australia, Parkes Place, Canberra, ACT 2600

State Library of New South Wales, Macquarie Street, Sydney, NSW 2000

State Library of South Australia, North Terrace, Adelaide, South Australia 5001

State Library of Victoria, 328 Swanston Street, Melbourne, Victoria 3000

Associations

Australasian Association of Genealogists and Record Agents (AAGRA), P.O. Box 268, Oakleigh, Victoria 3166
Also conducts research in New Zealand.

Australasian Federation of Family History Organisations, c/o Richmond Villas, 120, Kent Street, Sydney, NSW 2000

Australian Institute of Genealogical Studies Inc., 6 Lavelle Street, Blackburn, Victoria 3130

Genealogical Society of Queensland, PO Box 8423, Woolloogabba, Queensland 4102

Genealogical Society of Victoria, 5th Floor, Curtin House, 252 Swanston Street, Melbourne, Victoria 3000

Irish Ancestry Group (IAG)
See Genealogical Society of Victoria.

Society of Australian Genealogists (SAG), Richmond Villas 120 Kent Street, Observatory Hill, Sydney, NSW 2000

Western Australia Genealogical Society Inc., 5/48, May Street, Bayswater, Western Australia 6053

Civil registration

Held by the relevant registry in each State. Public record offices hold microfiche copies of indexes for public use.

Tasmania

Archives

Archives Office of Tasmania, 91 Murray Street, Hobart

New Zealand

Archives

National Archives of New Zealand, Archives House, 5 Malgrave Street, Wellington
Postal address: PO Box 6148, Wellington 6035

Associations

Genealogical Research Institute of New Zealand (GRINZ), P.O. Box 36–107, Moera, Lower Hutt

New Zealand Society of Genealogists Inc., P.O. Box 8795, Symonds Street, Auckland 1035

Civil registration

Registrar General of New Zealand, Levin House, Lower Hutt

South Africa

Archives

The Chief Archivist, Cape (State) Archives, Private Bag X 9025, Capetown, Cape 8000

Associations

Genealogical Society of South Africa, P.O. Box 1344, Kelvin, Transvaal 2054

Civil registration

The Director-General, Home Affairs, Division of Births, Deaths, Marriages, Private Bag X 114, Pretoria, Transvaal 0001

Appendix C

RECORDS AND THEIR SOURCES

This section is a quick reference to the records and sources described in this book. It directs readers to the appropriate chapters, enabling them to speedily identify the repositories concerned. The address of each source will be found in Appendix B. Non-Irish material is included where this is considered relevant.

Abreviations used

AOT	Archives Office of Tasmania
ASA	Australian State Archives
BL	British Library, London
DGHA	Director General, Home Affairs, South Africa
FRC	Family Records Centre
GO	Genealogical Office, Dublin
GRO	General Register Office, Dublin
GRONI	General Register Office of Northern Ireland
GSV	Genealogical Society of Victoria, Australia
IGRS	Irish Genealogical Research Society, London
IPS	Irish Philatelic Society, Dublin
Local	Libraries, societies, heritage centres in Ireland
MOR	Mormon family history centres worldwide
NA	National Archives, Dublin
NANZ	National Archives of New Zealand
NAW	National Archives, Washington DC, USA
NEWS	British Library Newspaper Library, London
NLI	National Library of Ireland, Dublin (BLNL)
NRH	New Register House, Edinburgh
NSW	New South Wales, Australia
PHS	Presbyterian Historical Society, Belfast
PRO	Public Record Office, London
PRONI	Public Record Office of Northern Ireland, Belfast
RCBL	Representative Church Body Library, Dublin
RD	Registry of Deeds, Dublin
RG	Registrar General, New Zealand
SFL	Society of Friends Library, Dublin and Lisburn
SLS	State Library, Sydney
SOG	Society of Genealogists, London

Record	Source	Chapter
Census returns		
Ireland (surviving 1821–1891)	NA; NLI; PRONI	6
All Ireland (1901/1911)	NA; local	6
England/Wales	FRC	4
Scotland	NRH	4
USA	Federal/State/county	4
Australia, 1828 Census of NSW	Published	4
Census substitutes		
Surveys, directories, local censuses, etc.	NA; NLI; PRONI; local	6
IGI	PRO; MOR	6
Civil registration		
All Ireland	GRO	6
N. Ireland	GRONI	6
Microfilmed indexes	MOR	6
England/Wales	FRC	4
Scotland	NRH	4
USA	State	4
Canada	Province	4
Australia	State	4
New Zealand	RG	4
South Africa	DGHA	4
Convicts		
Irish transportation records (1788–1868)	NA; SLS	4
Convict transport registers (1867)	PRO	4
NSW original correspondence	PRO	4
Convict material	ASA	4
Index of convict names	GSV	4
Musters for NSW and Tasmania (from 1788)	SLS; AOT	4
Deeds		
Memorials of mortgages, leases, wills, etc.	RD	6
Indexes	RD; NLI	6
Documents		
Anglo-Norman era	NA	5
Estate papers		
Republic of Ireland	NA; NLI; local	6
N. Ireland	PRONI	6
Griffith's Valuation		
Ireland	NA; NLI; VO; PRONI; local	6
Britain	BL; IGRS; SOG	6

Record	Source	Chapter
Immigrants to New South Wales (assisted)		
Records	SLS	4
Index (1840–1870)	SLS	4
Newspapers		
Ireland	NLI; local	4
Britain (from 1822)	NEWS	4
Australia (ships, passengers BM&D notices)	NSW Archives (for period 1803–1842)	4
New Zealand (pre-1876 D&M notices)	NANZ	4
Orphans		
To Australia	ASA	4
Owners of Land (1873)		
Ireland	NA	6
Britain	BL; PRO; county record offices	6
Parish records		
Church of Ireland	NA; PRONI; RCBL; parishes	6
Roman Catholic	NLI; PRONI; parishes	6
Presbyterian	local ministers; PHS; PRONI; NA	6
Quaker records	SFL; PRONI	6
Royal Irish Constabulary		
Personnel records	NA; PRO	6
Poor Law records		
Ireland	NA; PRONI; local	4
Britain	County record offices	4
Shipping		
Outward passenger lists (1890-1960)	PRO	4
Emigrants and cabin passengers to NZ (1839–1850)	PRO	4
Passenger arrival lists (copies/extracts 1820–1905)	NAW	4
Immigration passenger lists (1883–1945)	NAW	4
Stamps		
Irish	Post offices; friends in Ireland; IPS	2
Tithes		
All Ireland	NA; local	6
N. Ireland	PRONI; local; IGRS	6

Record	Source	Chapter
Townland Index		
Ireland	NA; NLI; PRONI; local	1
Britain	BL; IGRS; PRO	1
Topographical Dictionary of Ireland		
Ireland	NA; NLI; PRONI; local	1
Britain	BL; IGRS	1
Valuation documents (land)		
Republic of Ireland	VO; NA	6
N. Ireland	PRONI	6
Wills		
Transcriptions/indexes/ abstracts (post-1858)	NA; RD	6
Will books (N. Ireland) (and card index)	PRONI	6
Other collections of wills and indexes	NLI; RD; GO	6
Workhouse records		
Ireland	NA; PRONI; local	4
Britain	County record offices	4

Appendix D

UNIVERSAL BIBLIOGRAPHY

For the convenience of readers, this section brings together the bibliographical lists that appear at the end of each chapter.

Adams, William Forbes, *Ireland and Irish Emigration To The New World,* Genealogical Publishing Co. Inc., Baltimore, 1980.

Alphabetical Index to the Townlands and Towns of Ireland 1871, British Parliamentary Papers HC 1877 XVI

Ancestor, Vol. 18, No. 3, Genealogical Society of Victoria, 1987.

Ancestor, Vol. 19, Nos. 3, 4, 7, Genealogical Society of Victoria, Australia, 1989.

Aspects of Irish Genealogy: Proceedings of the First Irish Genealogical Congress, First Irish Genealogical Committee, Dublin.

Bagley, Gary Allen et al., *Basic Irish Genealogical Sources. Description and Evaluation,* Ontario Genealogical Society, Ottawa, 1993.

Beckett, J.C., *The Making of Modern Ireland 1603–1923,* Faber and Faber, London, reprinted 1989.

Bell, Russ, Australian Connection, *Family Tree Magazine,* Vol. 4, No. 3, 1988.

Bell, Russ, The First Settlement in Australia, *Family Tree Magazine,* Vol. 4, No. 7, 1988.

Bellam, Michael, The Irish in New Zealand, *Familia,* Vol. 2, No. 1, Ulster Historical Foundation, Belfast, 1985.

Bevan, Amanda and Duncan, Andrea, *Tracing Your Ancestors in The Public Record Office,* HMSO, London, 4th edn., 1990.

Births and Deaths Registration (Ireland) Act 1863

Blarney, Vol. 3, No. 3, Irish Ancestry Group Inc., 1991 (an inaugural member society of the GSV).

Brackpool, Marion, A Peep Into My Mailbag, *Journal of the East Surrey Family History Society,* Vol. 11, No. 1, 1988.

Bradley, Ann Kathleen, *History of The Irish in America,* Chartwell Books, New Jersey, 1986.

British Parliamentary Papers 1800–1900, (1000 volume series), Irish University Press (Irish Academic Press Ltd.), Dublin, 1977.

Brown, Frances, 'Notes From the State Library of Victoria', *The Genealogist,* Vol. VII, No. 4, Australian Institute of Genealogical Studies, Victoria, 1992.

Camp, Anthony, *Sources for Irish Genealogy in the Society of Genealogists,* Society of Genealogists, London, 1990.

Chiswell, Ann V., Convicts Destined for New South Wales, Australia, *Family Tree Magazine,* Vol. 4, No. 3, 1988.

Cockton, Peter, *Subject Catalogue of the House of Commons Parliamentary Papers 1801–1900,* Chadwyck-Healy Ltd., Cambridge, 1988.

Connell, K.H., *The Population of Ireland 1750–1845,* Clarendon Press, Oxford, 1950.

Costello, Con, *Botany Bay,* Mercier Press, Dublin, 1987.

Currer-Briggs, Noel, *Worldwide Family History,* Routledge and Kegan Paul, 1982.

Dear, Robert B., Samuel Speed, the Last Convict in Australia, *Family Tree Magazine,* Vol. 7, No. 11, 1991.

Dictionary of South African Biography, Cape edition 1906, Transvaal edition 1905.

Ellis, Peter Beresford, *Hell or Connaught,* Blackstaff Press, Belfast, reprinted 1989.

Families, Vol. 32, No. 4, Ontario Genealogical Society, Toronto, Ontario, 1993.

Family History News and Digest, Vols. 7–9, Federation of Family History Societies, Birmingham.

ffolliott, Rosemary, Irish Census Returns and Census Substitutes, *Irish Genealogy: A Record Finder,* Heraldic Artists Ltd., Dublin, 1987.

ffolliott, Rosemary, The Registry of Deeds for Genealogical Purposes, *Irish Genealogy: A Record Finder,* Heraldic Artists Ltd., Dublin, 1987.

ffolliott, Rosemary and O'Byrne, Eileen, Wills and Administrations, *Irish Genealogy: A Record Finder,* Heraldic Artists Ltd., Dublin, 1987.

Filby, P. William, North American Passenger Lists, *ISBGFH Newsletter,* Vol. 11, No. 3, 1982.

Filby, P. William and Lower, Dorothy M. (ed.), *Passenger and Immigration Lists Index 1992, Supplement: A Guide to Published Arrivals Records of More Than 2,029,000 Passengers Who Came to the New World,* Gale Research 1992.

The Genealogist, Vol. VII, No. 9, Australian Institute of Genealogical Studies, Victoria, 1994.

The General Alphabetical Index to the Townlands and Towns, Parishes and Baronies of Ireland, Alexander Thom, Dublin, 1861, reprinted 1984 by Genealogical Publishing Co. Inc., Baltimore, Massachusetts, USA.

General Report of the Census of Ireland 1901, British Parliamentary Papers HC 1902 CXXIX.

General Report of the Census of Ireland 1911, British Parliamentary Papers HC 1912–13 CXVIII.

Gillen, Mollie, *The Founders of Australia,* Library of Australian History, Sydney, 1989.

Glazier, Ira, *The Famine Immigrants 1846–51,* Genealogical Publishing Company, Baltimore, 1983.

Gorry, Paul, Irish Genealogical Congress, *Family Tree Magazine,* Vol. 7, No. 2, 1990.

Gorry, Paul, Guidebook Guide, *Irish Roots,* No. 4, Belgrave Publications, Cork, 1992.

Gorry, Paul, Guidebook Guide, *Irish Roots,* No. 2, Belgrave Publications, Cork, 1993.

Grenham, John, *Tracing Your Irish Ancestors,* Gill and MacMillan, Dublin, 1992.

Griffin, William D., *The Irish in America 550–1972,* Oceana Publications Inc., New York, 1973.

Griffin, William D., *A Portrait of the Irish in America,* Charles Scribner's Sons, New York, 1981.

Guide to Genealogical Research in the National Archives (Canada), National Archives Trust Fund Board.

Guide to the Public Record Office of Northern Ireland, PRONI, Belfast, 1991.

Hadden, Gordon William, South African Research, *ISBGFH,* Vol. 11, No. 4, 1989.

Hawkings, D. *Bound For Australia,* Phillimore, Chichester, 1987.

Hayes, Richard J., *Manuscript Sources for the History of Irish Civilisation,* G.K. Hall, Boston, Massachusetts, 1965.

Hickey, D.J and Doherty, J.E., *A Dictionary of Irish History 1800–1980,* Gill and MacMillan, Dublin, reprinted 1989.

Holden, Keith, Aspects of Convict Research and Records, *Ancestor,* Vol. 19, No. 3, 1988.

Hughes, R., *The Fatal Shore,* London, 1987.

The Irish Genealogist, Irish Genealogical Research Society, London.

James, Alwyn, *Scottish Roots,* MacDonald Publishers, Midlothian, Scotland, reprinted 1988.

Janine, Roy, *Tracing Your Ancestors in Canada,* Minister of Supply and Services, Canada, 9th edn., 1988.

Johnson, W. Branch, *The English Prison Hulks,* Phillimore, Chichester, revised edition, 1970.

Kelly, M.J. My Projects, *The New Zealand Genealogist,* Vol. 21, No. 206, 1990.

Kyle, Noeline, *Tracing Family History in Australia,* Methuen, Australia, 1985.

The Landed Gentry, National Library of Ireland, Dublin, 1979.

The Land War 1879–1903, National Library of Ireland, Dublin, 1976.

Lewis, Samuel, *Topographical Dictionary of Ireland,* London, 1837.

McCarthy, Tony (Ed.), *Irish Roots,* Issues 1 and 2, Belgrave Publications, Cork, 1993.

McCarthy, Tony, *The Irish Roots Guide,* Lilliput Press, Dublin, 1991.

McClaughlin, Trevor, Barefoot and Pregnant? Female Orphans who Emigrated from Irish Workhouses to Australia 1848–50, *Familia,* Vol. 2, No. 3, Ulster Historical Foundation, 1985.

McCracken, Donal P, The Irish in South Africa. The Police, A Case Study, *Familia,* Vol. 2, No. 7, Ulster Genealogical and Historical Guild, 1991.

McDowell, R.B., *The Irish Administration 1801–1914,* Routledge and Keegan Paul, 1964.

McTernan, John C., *Sligo. Sources of Local History,* Sligo County Library, 1988.

Maher, Brian, Ireland Over Here. 19th Century Irish Immigrants in Southern New South Wales, *The Irish Australians,* Joint publication of the Society of Australian Genealogists and Ulster Historical Foundation, 1984.

Maitland, W.H., *The History of Magherafelt,* Moyola Books, Co. Londonderry, reprinted 1988.

The Manchester Genealogist, Vol. 25, No. 3, Manchester and Lancashire Family History Society, 1989.

The Manchester Genealogist, Vol. 30, No. 1, Manchester and Lancashire Family History Society, 1994.

Marriages (Ireland) Act 1844

Men of the Times, South Africa, Cape edition 1906, Transvaal edition 1905.

Morris, Richard B. *Encyclopaedia of American History.*

Newsleaf, Vol. 18, No. 1, Ontario Genealogical Society Supplement, Toronto, Ontario, 1988.

The New Zealand Genealogist, Vol. 22, No. 208, New Zealand Society of Genealogists, Auckland, 1991.

The New Zealand Genealogist, Vol. 24, No. 221, New Zealand Society of Genealogists, Auckland, 1993.

Nolan, William, *Tracing the Past. Sources for Local Studies in the Republic of Ireland,* Geography Publications, Dublin, 1982.

North Clare Wonderland, Leader Tourism Promotions, Lisdoonvarna, Co. Clare.

O'Neill, Capt. Francis (Ed.), *O'Neill's Music of Ireland,* Dan Collins, New York, 1963.

Prochaska, Alice, *Irish History from 1700. A Guide to Sources in the Public Record Office,* British Records Association, London, 1986.

Programme: First Irish Genealogical Congress 1991, Congress Office, Dublin, 1991.

Public Record Office Current Guide: Parts 1–3, HMSO, London.

Registration of Marriages (Ireland) Act 1863

Reid, Richard, From Ballyduff to Boorowa. Irish Assisted Immigration to New South Wales 1830–1896, *The Irish Australians,* Joint publication of the Society of Australian Genealogists and Ulster Historical Foundation, 1984.

Return of Owners of Land of One Acre and Upwards in Counties, Cities and Towns in Ireland, British Parliamentary Papers HC 1876 LXXX.

Return of Owners of Land of One Acre and Upwards in Counties, Cities and Towns in Ireland, Alexander Thom, Dublin, 1876, reprinted 1988 by Genealogical Publishing Co. Inc., Baltimore, Massachusetts.

Sainty, M.R. and Johnson, K.A. (Eds.), *Census of New South Wales. November 1828,* Library of Australian History, Sydney, 1980.

Sea Breezes, Vol. 68, No. 581, Kinglish Ltd., Douglas, Isle of Man, 1994.

Sharon, Margaret M., Kamloops Family History Society Seminar, *The British Columbia Genealogist,* Vol. 22, No. 2, British Columbia Genealogical Society, Canada, 1993.

Short Guide to the National Archives, National Archives, Dublin.

Sources for Family History and Genealogy, National Archives, Dublin, 1988.

You an Your Record Office A Code of Practice for Family Historians, Association of County Archivists in conjunction with the Federation of Family History Societies, 2nd edn., 1990.

The Voyage of Henry John Ford from London to Queensland, *Generation,* Vol. 16, No. 3, Genealogical Society of Queensland, 1994.

Western Ancestor, Vol. 4, No. 12, Western Australian Genealogical Society, 1990.

Woodham-Smith, Cecil, *The Great Hunger,* Hamish Hamilton, London, reprinted 1988.

Vine-Hall, Nick, Have You Australian Connections?, *Family Tree Magazine Yearbook,* Cambridgeshire, 1986.

INDEX

Gorry, Paul, 11, 77
Government policy on emigration, 22
Griffin, William, 20
Griffith's valuation, 36, 38, 51, 70
–, notebooks, 57
Grosse Isle, 18, 20
–, monuments, 20

Handwriting, legibility of, 8
Henry, Lt., 24
Heritage centres, 76, 79
History, local centres, 74
Hobson, William, 24
Host country, research in, 69
Householders' Index, 51
Hulks, 16, 21
–, *Essex,* 22
Surprise, 22

IGI, 63
Immigrants, selection of, 22
International reply coupons (IRCs), *see* Correspondence
Independence, American War of, 21
Institute of Heraldic and Genealogical Studies, 12
International Genealogical Index (IGI), 63
Internet, the, 76
Interviewing relatives, 6
Ireland, contacts in, 73
–, visiting, 72
Irish Ancestry Group, 70
Irish, discrimination against, 16, 20
Irish Genealogical Congress, 1st and 2nd, 77
Irish Genealogical Research Society (IGRS), 40
Irish Genealogist, The, 70
Irish in Britain, information about, 71
Irish Interests Directory, 70
Irish language 44
Irish records, availability, 1, 44
–, destruction of, 1, 33
–, limitations, 67
Irish research, basic knowledge of, 2, 69
–, conferences, 77

–, effect of old age upon, 8
–, preparations for, 2, 72
–, tourism, 1, 76, 77
Irish Roots Magazine, 72, 77
Irish stamps, how to obtain them, 11
Irish traditional music, 20

Kerry Bog Village, 74
Kings County, 5

Land, convict landowners, 24
–, gentry, 5, 74
–, landlords, 16, 74
–, owners of, 59
–, valuation, 51, 57, 70
Landed Estates 51
Language, Irish, 44
Laois, 5
Leix, 5
Letters, *see* Correspondence
Libraries, in Ireland, 73
–, reference (worldwide), 70
Library of Congress, 41
Liverpool 16, 17, 18
Locations, pinpointing of, 2
Londonderry, 5
Lovat, Fr., 24

McTernan, John C., 74
Male line, 6
Manuscript sources 51
Maps, Ordnance Survey, 39, 57
Microfiche, *Griffith's Valuation,* 56
–, *Tithe Applotments,* 57
Monaghan, 5
Montreal, 18
Monuments to Irish immigrants, 20
Mormon Church, and Irish records, 63
Music, Irish traditional, 20

Natal Mounted Police, 25
National Archives (NA), 33
National Archives of Canada, 42
National Library of Ireland (NLI), 34
New York, 16, 18, 20